MAKE EVERYTHING NEW

A Project on Communism

Edited by
Grant Watson
Gerrie van Noord
Gavin Everall

BOOK WORKS / PROJECT ARTS CENTRE

M. EVERYTHING NEW
A Project on Communism

CONTENTS

Can you explain a bit about your decision to use the term communism, a term, which is seen by many as redundant.

To talk about communism is to try to 'rescue communism from its own disrepute.'[1] To talk about it is also to depart from normative thinking and flirt with a position that is beyond the spectrum of everyday politics, a position that is perhaps untenable but at least one that shifts thinking away from its centre of gravity. A political climate in which neo-liberal capitalism has been able to 'invent the standards by which it is judged,'[2] partly through the conscious suppression of communism as a legitimate idea. If you read *The Communist Manifesto*, it comes across as if it was written today, and then there are many other communist-inspired thinkers whose work provides a set of critical tools with which to pick apart the dominant ideology and to question the widely held view that there is no alternative.

So does this mean that you are a communist?

In using the term communism, you don't necessarily need to label yourself a communist. Perhaps a different term would be more appropriate, but insisting on rigorously held positions and political labels is not the point. If these terms are compelling then why not pick them up and see what agency they have? Here the term communism is used in relation to contemporary art. And because it is a strong word but also sort of an intangible one, it has the effect of interpolating these works into a highly suggestive narrative and it gives them a generalised political colouring, which can appear in different circumstances as both abstract and concrete.

Hmm, that sounds quite vague. What is it exactly that you hope to achieve and are you in danger of evacuating the term of meaning? Or is this simply radical posturing?

That's a good point. If we were living in an environment where the term communism was actually outlawed, and to use it was to potentially face serious consequences, then there would be an immediate political agency stemming from its use. But instead we are living in a situation where it is possible to say almost anything. The only thing that is seemingly impossible is for these words to effect a radical transformation, which makes for a general sense of disengagement. In this context talk of communism can becoms nothing more than diverting background chatter – and therefore it is important to think about how this can best be avoided.

In the past communism always had a cultural wing, which meant that there was a continuity between political work and the work of artists and designers, actors, film-makers and so forth. People saw this work as one and the same. Perhaps what you should do is place yourself in the service of existing communist movements?

But would that synchronicity make sense today? Even during the period you speak of there were disagreements about what it was to make committed art, with different positions famously being argued by figures on the left such as

Adorno, Brecht, Lukács and Benjamin. in his text Alberto Toscano looks at the entangled relationship between politics and aesthetics and suggests Ranciere's division of the sensible as an ontological schema with which to approach this question. Given a reluctance to subsume art within the terms of a different category, this schema can be used to identify the 'ways of doing and making' [3] that constitute art's own immanent politics and it's ability to configure the world into objects, actions, modes of visibility, manners of speech and ways of being. And how, within the aesthetic domain, there is already the potential to form relationships and nodes of intersection with politics proper. Not to retreat from the world but instead to maintain the tension and interplay between these different categories and to develop a methodology that is critical and receptive to their intersecting points.

Apart from art, what about contemporary communist movements, do you relate to their cause in more general terms?

It's hard to say because these movements are varied and exist in relation to so many different circumstances. But a problem with traditional politics as Agamben points out, is that to overthrow power, without overthrowing the structures of power, is to chart a course towards the 'reef on which the revolutions' of preceding centuries 'have been shipwrecked.' [4] In other words, radical change has to be about more than regime change (although this may be necessary). It also has to address the micro-fascisms and the nature of sovereignty that stitches together our sense of being and binds it to power, whose most concrete form is the state and the law. And so, a new politics would have to 'open the field to a non-statal and non-juridical politics and human life – a politics and a life that are yet to be entirely thought.' [5] Maybe this politics will be called communism. Perhaps it will look like art.

So what about this book?

The book is part of a series of projects that address the term communism. And when it comes to a universal term like that, you have to be realistic and careful not to bite off more than you can chew. The solution has been to turn it into a collective question and to propose it to others. First there was an exhibition called *Communism*, which by working with a range of artists, functioned as a sampling process. Alongside there was a seminar, giving it its discursive co-ordinates. This book will be published at the same time as a series of radio broadcasts, and in the future there are plans to organise a further manifestation of the project that shifts this question into a very different geographic frame of reference. Along the way a constituency of participants has been built up, a constituency that is not too tightly defined, but that has evolved from a proximity of interests, a broadly shared disciplinary field (art) and in some instances an informal network of personal and professional relationships. For this book (as in the other projects), our suggestion for contributors was to think about how communism could be realised today and in response some artists proposed projects that spoke directly of a practical or symbolic realignment of the present. For example Maria Eichhorn's bank account that is open to all comers, or the use of collage as a cut and paste polemic in the work of CK Rajan, and as phantasmagoria and potentiality in the work of Klaus Weber. But many also looked to the past for inspiration. Sometimes taking in a grand historical sweep, like Michael Blum, whose film transcript is crowded with events and characters, or Wu Ming whose account reveals communism's linguistic roots.

Several of these contributions refer back to the 1960s and 1970s. Why do you think that this period is of particular interest to a current generation and what marks it out from the other so called revolutionary moments?

As Guattari and Negri said, 'It is not necessary to sit around in a café to realise that the cycle of revolution reopened in 1968.' [6] Gopal Balakrishnan also identifies this moment as a break with the pattern that earlier rebellions had established – and the use of the term 'cycle' suggests that we are still caught up in the dynamic that this period set in motion. It has a fascination for us today because it was a time when many new models emerged, new ways of living and artistic forms that had political implications and that tested the relationship between individual agency and the collective good. In his essay Rob Stone describes the way the composer Cornelius Cardew developed the Scratch Orchestra. The orchestra principally performed Cardew's works, but during the time it took for people to arrive and tune up, there was a free-form session where the musicians improvised from their own notations, which included text instructions, diagrams, drawings, found images and collage. The aim was to interpret each individual score whilst at the same time working towards a single sonic space (a singularity). It is interesting that Cardew eventually turned his back on the Scratch Orchestra, which he came to see as a harmless political burlesque, a side show of anarchic posturing and theatricality cut-off from real politics. He joined a communist party and wrote protest songs instead, which was his clear-cut answer to the question that we talked of earlier.

Given what you have just said about individual agency versus the group, do you think that by looking at exemplary figures you become too concerned with a romantic/heroic version of history?

No because in this book and as in many other contexts the exemplary figure can act as a 'stand in' for the group. Walter Benjamin calls this figure the 'righteous man' or a 'moral improvisation' that is both collectively performed and collectively owned 'and because no one is up to this role, it keeps changing hands.'[7] One example is Bengali novelist Mahasweta Devi's character Bashai Tudu, who is repeatedly captured and killed by the police but reappears again at the centre of fresh insurrections, becoming a mythical figure for his community to rally around. But sometimes these individuals become so diffused that they mutate and are lost to their original cause. This is arguably the case with Che Guevara whose face was cast into iconic relief by the Irish artist Jim Fitzpatrick. In a conversation with Aleksandra Mir, the two track this face as it shifts its terms of reference from private individual to freedom fighter to a visual franchise which is reproduced endlessly on T-shirts and the like. Sometimes an individual narrative leads by a circuitous route to a group scenario. So AA Bronson's trek across Canada and his experimentation with different types of behaviour and different ideas of community becomes the prelude to another chapter, the gathering together of the ideas, which will eventually be channelling into General Idea. Conversely an account of developments in society can intimate private lives. I am thinking of Martha Rosler's history of progressive politics and social struggle in New York that is inflected with anecdotes and autobiographical detail. Perhaps it is a romantic view of history, but for me the value of these stories is that they become part of a counter-narrative, the production of an alternative mythology that can be taken up and used – a mythology that is always 'flexible and in motion.'[8]

Perhaps by relating these stories and talking of mythology what you are getting at is a sort of poetics of communism. In which case my question would be about the value of small gestures that operate in a relatively contained field of activity. Taken as given the critiques of grand gestures and the problem with top down politics, don't you think that these gestures look feeble in the face of an ever-intensifying neo-liberal capitalism?

But small gestures have a tendency to multiply. Capitalism itself is a set of small ideas and simple procedures originating from a particular class that have run amok and given birth to something big, like an 'empty machine, working at full power'[9] – a machine that is more creative and flexible than anything that went before it, that thrives on conflict, and that carries within it the traces of all the revolutions past which it has consumed. Of course the question of agency becomes opaque when dissent is so easily assimilated, when you live in a system from which there is no exit. So perhaps it is about trying to figure out ways to inhabit this system differently, to get inside the machine and tinker with its parts. Maybe it's not a question of another world is possible but rather another world already exists – only it must be identified and reclaimed. After all, secreted inside this machine and oiling its parts, is the real capital on which prosperity and development are built. Those 'products of the co-operation between minds' such as 'knowledge, language, science, culture, art, information, forms of life, relations with oneself, with others and the world'[10] which have been purloined from the common good and brought to market.

And how does the work of artists come into this equation?

Maurizio Lazzarato, who coined some of the terms used above, takes the figure of the conceptual artist to illustrate his point. He argues that within an economy of ideas, common goods are 'realised like the modalities that Marcel Duchamp used, to speak about artistic creation. A work of art is indeed for one half the result of the activity of the artist and for the other half the result of the activity of the public (which looks at it, reads it, or listens to it)' – and the products of this transaction are free.[11] They are the result of 'co-creation' and because they are infinite 'the one who transmits them does not lose them, does not suffer by socialising them, but, on the contrary, their value increases in the organisation of their diffusion and sharing.'[12] Despite the obvious fact that art is embedded within commodity culture, there is a part of it that always functions within a communism of ideas. A mode of production and distribution that treats the general intellect as a collective resource, that goes beyond the level of entertainment and commodity, the level of persuasion or propaganda even, to the place where concepts are invented. It can define this place and gives these concepts shape – a way of being in the world.

But what about the urgent steps needed to confront the very real physical destruction that capitalism is causing? How can such cultural gestures locate themselves or align themselves in a way that allows them to have a practical effect?

This is a tough question because of the order of magnitude we are dealing with. Yes alignments are a strategic way of building critical mass and often with artists these alignments start with the pooling of resources amongst themselves, as in the many collectives and artists' groups operating today. Some of which are represented here, such as Raqs Media Collective, Dmitry Gutov's Lifshitz Institute, Factotum, 16Beaver, Wu Ming, Ultra-red and The Metropolitan Complex.

Then individual artists and groups can expand the network to include other affiliations. Some that are political or activist and others that constitute more unlikely conjunctions, the previously un-thought associations that art is so good at making, often in the moment, and often as a matter of contingency. Artists also have a keen understanding of the event and the tension that is generated when gestures fine-tuned to the need of a particular moment, to its points of 'conjuncture', the nodal points where 'relations of force' come together.[13]

And where does this emphasis on the moment leave your romantic view of history?

Here in the present, because to make everything new is not to conjure something out of thin air, but to wilfully take fragments of the past from their historical context (rearrange them) and put them to work in the present, produce new effects out of old things, which with 'a small displacement' brings them full cycle.[14]

So, is that what you mean by revolution?

Yes, because, the term 'revolution' is not only one of novelty, but also an astronomical term, 'designating the regular, lawfully revolving motion of the stars,' and indicating 'a recurring cyclical movement.'[15]

NOTES.
1. Félix Guattari and Antonio Negri, 'Communists Like Us', *Semiotext(e)*, Columbia University Press, New York,1990, p. 7.

2. Gopal Balakrishnan, 'Future Unknown', *New Left Review*, London, 2005

3. Jaqcues Rancière, *The Politics of Aesthetics*, Continuum, London, 2005, p.13.

4. Giorgio Agamben, *Means Without Ends, Notes on Politics*, Minnesota Press, Minneapolis, 2000, p. 111.

5. Giorgio Agamben, *Homo Sacer*

Sovereign Power and Bare Life, Stanford University Press, California, 1998, p. 12.

6. Félix Guattari and Antonio Negri, p. 20.

7. Walter Benjamin, *Illuminations*, Trans. Harry Zohn, Jonathan Cape, London, 1982.

8. Wu Ming, *Infopool* No.7, www.infopool.org.uk, 2003, p. 4.

9. Maurizio Lazzarato, term used as part of a lecture organised by Wiels Contemporary Art Centre, Brussels, 2006.

10. Maurizio Lazzarato, 'From Capital – Labour to Capital – Life, Ephemera | Theory of the Multitude', www.ephemeraweb.org, 2004, p. 13.

11. Ibid.

12. Ibid.

13. Louis Althusser, *Machiavelli and Us*, Verso, London, 1999, p. 19.

14. Walter Benjamin, *Illuminations*.

15. Hannah Arendt, *On Revolution*, Penguin, London, 1990, p. 220.

THE MU PARTICLE IN 'COMMUNISM'
Wu Ming

So you want us to send a contribution about Communism.

Not about any group of people calling themselves communists.

Not about any one of the countless currents of 'Communism'.

Not about operetta nation-states like Laos and North Korea.

No, you're talking about the core concept of Communism. You want us to dig and touch the roots.

Thanks to commies and anti-commies, Communism seems to be today's most unpopular, outdated, crestfallen issue.

The very term was bad-mouthed, adulterated, clumsified, claw-hammered out of public discourse.

Time to deal with it again.

The word *Kommunismus/Communismus* was coined as a neologism (both in German and late Latin), and sporadically employed in a derogatory way during and after the religious wars that set Europe on fire from the Late Middle Ages to Early Modernity. The doctrines of sixteenth-century radical currents such as the Hutterites, the Hussites and the Taborites were described as *communisticae* by some of their coeval enemies and later detractors. Then the word was engulfed, until it sensationally re-emerged in the nineteenth-century.

All those sixteenth-century heresies proclaimed sharing of goods and communal living, and some of them advocated forced expropriation of the nobility and the clergy. During the German Peasants' War (1524-1525), a chain of riotous events that sent waves of rebellion across Central Europe, one of preacher Thomas Müntzer's battle cries was *Omnia sunt communia*, all things are common. It should go without saying that such an emphasis on sharing was deeply rooted in Christian history and doctrine. '*Erant illis omnia communia*' (Act 4,32): 'Things were in common among them'. And the Rule of St. Augustine (ca. 400 AC) says: 'Et non dicatis aliquid proprium, sed sint vobis omnia communia': 'Call nothing your own, but let everything be yours in common'.

Commūnis. Let's take a close look at this Latin adjective. *Commūnis* means 'common', 'universal', 'generally shared'. *Mūnĭa* means 'duties', 'public offices', 'tolls', 'excises', and any kind of civil services and obligations to the community. Therefore, *Cum mūnis* means 'with duties', 'with dues', 'with engagements', i.e. obliged to take part in the life of a regulated community. Curiously enough, the antonym of *Commūnis* is *Immūnis*, which means 'with no duties', 'free from engagements', 'free of tax'.[1]

This is just the beginning of the journey back, for the word *Mn a* itself has a very long history. The ancient root *'Mai'/'Mau'/'Mu'* has to do with calculating, weighing, measuring things – presumably in order to exchange them equitably or distribute them between your fellow persons. That's what supposed to happen with duties in a fairly regulated community. We can find this correspondence in several ancient languages. In Vedic Sanskrit, the 4000-year-old sacred language of India, *Mâti* means 'to measure'. In Latin, *Mensio* means 'measure' (French: *Mesure*; Italian: *Misura*). In Old Slavonic (the first literary Slavic language, developed in the ninth century) *Mena* means 'exchange', 'barter'. In Old Lithuanian (fifteenth century), *Maínas* has the same meaning. In Germanic languages, there was a distinct but parallel terminological evolution: the German adjective *Gemeinas* perfectly reflects *Commūnis*. *Ge-meinas = Cum-mūnis*.[2] That's also where the English words *Moon* (Greek: *Mnvn*; Gothic:[3] *Mēna*; Old English:[4] *Mōna*) and *Month* (Greek: *Mnv*, Latin: *Mensis*) come from. The moon was used in order to count days and measure longer periods of time. That's also where *Mind* (Latin: *Mens*) comes from. The mind is the organ that counts/measures/weighs and then sets the value and the *meaning* of things. Of course, the word *Meaning* has the same origins.

Most important, the Akkadian word *Manû* means 'to count on the fingers'.[5] Akkadian is an ancient Semitic language. It was already widely spoken (and written in cuneiform) in Mesopotamia 4,500 years ago. It was the language of that era's 'international' commerce. Plenty of inscriptions and tablets have been found all over Asia Minor.

The most prestigious and controversial Italian linguist and philologist, the late Giovanni Semerano (1913-2005), devoted his entire life to tracing the origins of all European languages back to Akkadian and a common Semitic base. He filled almost all the gaps in the etymology of Greek and Latin terms. We're drawing heavily from his works and discoveries.[6]

Let's go further back now. What is the reason the root *'Mai'* / *'Mau'*/*'Mu'* has to do with measuring and sharing? The Akkadian term for 'water' is *Mû*. Ugaritic:[7] *Mj*. Aramaic:[8] *Majjā*. Water is the most valuable resource, you can barter anything for it if you're thirsty. Water is the mainstay of any community, the first thing that must be shared equally. The necessity of distributing and sharing water is the precondition and basis of all economy and social regulation. We're sinking deep into the past, speculating on the very birth of human language. There's a strict correspondence between the

consonant 'M' and water. The sound 'M' is roughly ono-
matopoeic of drinking. If you're thirsty and get to drink
avidly, you emit a deep, low sound that can be rendered
as 'Oom... Oom... Oom...' In Italian baby-speak, the word
for 'water' is Bumba (pronounced '*Boom-bah*').

Finally, we can say that the '-*mu(n)*' par-
ticle contained in the word 'Com-munism' has to do with
water. Which has now become the scarcest of resources.
If the word were refreshed, recharged, revamped, its
return to use couldn't be better timed.

NOTES.
1. If the antonym of 'Common' is 'Immune', then Communism is the ideology of 'nonimmunity', and it's true that 'Communism is a disease of the mind', as American journalist and moral crusader George Putnam said on 23 October 1966. It was one of the punch lines in his commemorative speech on the 1956 Hungarian uprising.

2. By the way, *Gemeinwesen* ('community', 'common essence', 'communal being') was one of Karl Marx's favourite words, as well as one of the key concepts in his early texts, e.g. the 'Critical Notes on the Article 'The King of Prussia and Social Reform. By a Prussian'.' (1844): 'But do not all rebellions without exception have their roots in the disasterous isolation of man from the *gemeinwesen*? Does not every rebellion necessarily presuppose isolation? Would the revolution of 1789 have taken place if French citizens had not felt disasterously isolated from the *gemeinwesen*? The abolition of this isolation was its very purpose. But the *gemeinwesen* from which the workers is isolated is a *gemeinwesen* of quite different reality and scope than the political *gemeinwesen*. The gemeinwesen from which his own labor separates him is life itself, physical and spiritual life, human morality, human activity, human enjoyment, human nature.'. As regards the development of this concept in twentieth century critical post-Marxism, see the works of French thinker Jacques Camatte.

3. Gothic was the Germanic language spoken by the Goths (2nd-5th Century). They later split into two different tribes, Ostrogoths and Visigoths, and practically took over the dying Roman Empire in Southern Europe.

4. By 'Old English' (also called 'Anglo-Saxon') linguists mean the Germanic language spoken in England before the 1066 Norman invasion.

5. It's the only reasonable etymo-

logical explanation of the Latin word *Manus*, 'hand'. Italian and Spanish: *Mano*; Portuguese: *Mão*; French: *Main*; Catalan: *Mà*.

6. Semerano's findings were systematized in his immense work *Le origini della cultura europea* [The Origins of European Culture] which was published in two 2-volume instalments whose subtitles are *Rivelazioni della linguistica storica* [Revelations from Historical Linguistics] (Olschki, Florence 1984, ISBN 8822232542) and *Basi semitiche delle lingue indo-europee* [The Semitic Foundations of Indo-European Languages] (Olschki, Florence 1994, ISBN 8822242335). In the following decade, he 'popularised' his theories in shorter books, and published further groundbreaking studies on the Etruscan language. His latest works include *La favola dell'indoeuropeo* [The Myth of the Indo-European Language] (B. Mondadori, Milan 2005, ISBN 8842492744) and *Il popolo che sconfisse la morte: Gli Etruschi e la loro lingua* [The People that Defeated Death: The Etruscans and their Language] (B. Mondadori, Milan 2006, ISBN 8842490709). As far as we know, there is no English translation of his books.

7. Ugaritic was a Semitic language spoken in Syria from the fourteenth through the twelfth century BC.

8. Aramaic is another Semitic language, very close to Hebrew, and Jesus of Nazareth's mother tongue, as it was the everyday language spoken by Jews in Palestine. At the time the region was part of the Roman empire. Aramaic and its dialects are still spoken in some parts of the Middle East (especially Syria). Some books of the Bible were originally written in Aramaic (e.g. the book of Daniel).

www.wumingfoundation.com

This text is licensed under a Creative Commons Attribution-Non Commercial-No Derivs 2.5 License.

Aleksandra Mir
Che and Concorde
poster design
2004 - 2005

NOT EVERYTHING
IS ALWAYS BLACK OR WHITE
Aleksandra Mir/Jim Fitzpatrick

A telephone conversation between the author of the collage, Aleksandra Mir (New York) and the creator of the original Che Guevara poster, Jim Fitzpatrick, (Dublin). 3 January 2005, 2pm EST.

Aleksandra Mir: A couple of communist neighbours in the Swedish neighbourhood where I grew up in the 1970s had your poster on their wall. Long before I could even begin to understand who Che Guevara was, I was blown away by the visual power of this image. It fed my hunger for visual culture and taught me a lot about composition and colour. Today, as a practising artist myself, I still find it to be the ultimate graphic ever created. For the last few years I have had it up on my own wall here in New York City, although with the slight alteration of a now defunct Concorde flying above Che's head. Could you describe the technical approach to your original graphic a little?

Jim Fitzpatrick: It's essentially just making a line dropout of a photograph. At the time (1967) I was doing a series for an Irish magazine called *Scene*. The editor commissioned me to do quite a radical series called 'A voice in our times', relating to the Vietnam War. It was very satirical. I used people's own words against them. I used Lyndon Johnson's words on Vietnam. Today you hear a lot about Blair as being Bush's 'poodle'. But I did Harold Wilson, the British Prime Minister at the time, as Lyndon Johnson's 'poodle'. The dog with his head out. Then I decided I wanted to be a bit more radical, and I did the Che Guevara image. Initially I was working in a very Art Noveau-ish style, like Beardsley, and the first image I did of Che was psychedelic, it looks like he is in seaweed. His hair was not hair, it was shapes that I felt gave it an extra dimension. That was the image I produced for the magazine and that was done before he died and that is the important thing about that image. At first it didn't print. It was considered far too strong and revolutionary. I was very inspired by Che's trip to Bolivia. He went there with the intent to overthrow the intensely corrupt government, helped by the Americans at the time, and that's where he died. I thought he was one of the greatest men who ever lived, and I still do in many ways. And when he was murdered, I decided I wanted to do something about it, so I created the poster. I felt this image had to come out, or he would not be commemorated otherwise, he would go where heroes go, which is usually into anonymity.

I thought my original psychedelic work was very artistic, very beautiful, but it didn't communicate the way the red and black did. It hit you in the face. For reference, I was looking at a photograph that I had seen in the German *Stern* magazine, a strong political magazine with left-wing views. It was a photo taken by Korda, but I didn't know that at the time. I had bought the magazine to try to learn a bit of German, and because I liked what it did, and in terms of graphics it was pretty far advanced as well. So I did a number of graphic versions from the photo. The first was a square, black and white. The second that I re-photographed had poster proportions, 20 x 30 inches.

You had made a second generation of your own image?

Yes. I made a paper negative on a piece of equipment I used to have that was called a 'Grant'. Have you ever heard of it?

No…?

It was like a giant light box. Anybody who worked in advertising, or with a printer in those days, before the age of computers, would know what it was. Essentially it made a big paper negative of anything you wanted. You put your image underneath it. I drew on acetate so the light could go through. You put a sheet of photographic paper on top of that, closed it, turned on the light box, developed it in developer and fixed it in fixer. It was very smelly and very messy. The third image was the black on red, because I had decided to do leaflets, everything, and hand them out to everybody. The red and black image was made in two flat colours, two separations. I re-drew the photograph, that's what I call a line dropout. I wanted it to look photographic but I drew it by hand, on Litho film. I wanted it to look stark so put it on a red background, but if you saw the artwork, all you saw was a flat black with a centre cut-out for the face. If you ever did silk-screening you know you work in black and white and then you print it in any colour you like, basically. So that was printed then in one colour black and one colour red, and I decided that the star should be yellow, so I painted that in with a magic marker.

By hand, all of them? What was the original edition of the poster?

Yeah. I think I printed 1000 and gave most of them away for free, I decided to get them into shops, not to make money, just to get them around. To be honest I don't even have one of them myself, for they all went all over the place. I was over in London a lot and I distributed them there. There was a huge demand for them. One lot went to Spain and they were seized by Franco's police.

Did you send them around haphazardly, or did you have designated recipients?

I would love to say it was well-organised, but it was quite haphazard. Friends of mine going to the continent would get a batch, a lot of odd people ended up distributing the work. What I was trying to do in a way was to get people to notice that this man had been murdered. It was a big story at the time but it faded away. I felt this was somebody exceptional. The poster was published in *Private Eye*, a famous satirical magazine that is still going. They passed it on to a guy called Peter Meyer, who was an art critic for *Studio International*, the most influential art magazine of its day. He was quite ecxited about it and along with other artists he invited us all to participate in an exhibition at the Lisson Gallery in London to commemorate Che Guevara. It didn't happen at the Lisson in the end, but in a space called the Arts Laboratory. This was happening at the same time that Yoko Ono was having her first exhibition, she'd met John Lennon. She was chopping her clothes off with a scissor. The exhibition was titled *Viva Che*. So for this show I did a number of works, first I silk-screened a black image and painted in the red by hand, to make it an original, and that was acrylic on board. They were going to sell the original to raise money. I also made an oil painting, a very big, black and white version, on canvas. That was more painterly, a heavy impasto for the whites.

You made a painting from your poster?

I made a painting of the poster.

Where is that now?

I'm gonna tell you now. Nowhere is the answer. The first psychedelic image I had made of Che was also part of this show. None of them ever came back or were returned. I was told they disappeared in Eastern Europe on tour somewhere. You would have to be a detective to find out what happened, I have some of the names of the people involved if you want to follow it up.

We'll do that next year. We'll track down your originals (laughs).

I would love to, the oil painting was magnificent. God knows, I don't know what happened to it all, it wasn't just me, lots of other artists were also working on their own images of Che Guevara.

But before you had these invitations, you just went about printing and distributing on your own? How did you finance and organise that?

I did it right out of my own pocket. I also had friends who were printers, one who today is one of the richest capitalists in Ireland, and very proud he printed it for me, but I had to pay for it. I just got a good price.

So after the first edition of the initial 1000, how did it gain mass distribution after that?

It really took off. There seemed to be a huge demand for it. I decided on that basis to form a poster company called Two Bear Feet. I produced the poster and a couple of psychedelic variations on it. My favourite was a black on silver foil board. So it was quite spectacular and I only did about a hundred that I gave away to my friends and people I was trying to impress. At that stage I was an artist looking for work and I handed it out. I made all these images copyright free. Not because I didn't know who the photographer was who took the picture at the time, but because I believed in the cause. I wanted anybody and everybody to copy it, change it, do whatever they bloody wanted to do with it.

So you didn't approach it as an illustrator, you were right in the middle of things, as an activist?

I was very much an activist. I was doing a lot of work for a left-wing political party called The Official IRA. They were the original IRA who downed arms, called a ceasefire and then became a political party. They were very much spied on by British Intelligence, army intelligence here, by just about everybody. I got stopped on the street quite a lot in those days. I always thought, 'What are they looking for? What are they going to do with posters?' I had made a number of posters for a group called People's Democracy in Northern Ireland, before everything went haywire, I worked for them for free. I did a lot of work free, I still do.

But you still always maintain a commercial practice next to that to support those activities, is that how it works?

Well, I do Celtic work, and I do album covers, I work for a band called The Darkness. I've done Sinéad O'Connor, and all of the Thin Lizzy's but The Darkness is one of the biggest bands in the world, they've sold more than 10 million copies.

So can you talk a little bit about copyright in general, because it appears that you embody two very different ideas about it.

I've made anything on my website free, you can download anything you like in high resolution for free. But I do point out that I own the copyright of the images, and that I don't mind people like yourself or ordinary people downloading them, printing them out, but if I find a big American company or English company stealing the images, I'd sue their ass off.

So you are adamant about copyright when it comes to commercial exploitation of your work, but you want to promote the idea of copyright free when it has a political purpose or popular distribution?

Absolutely.

That's interesting and that echoes Korda's sentiments as well.

Korda has said that I was the one who made his photograph famous. I actually have in my possession a signed photograph, the Che Guevara photograph, signed by Korda. I am very proud of that. I had no wish to stop him from earning money. Do you know the story of the Che Guevara image itself?

Yeah, I've done quite a lot of research on it.

So you know the story of the Italian publisher Feltrinelli. (Giangiacomo) Feltrinelli stole the photograph, and he made a lot of money from it. And he never gave any money to Korda. I don't want to get into the politics of it cause I was threatened by him a long time ago. He is dead now. But he was one of the Brigado Rosso, Red Brigade leaders. You know all of this?

I know some of it. You are filling in some of my blanks and maybe I can fill in some of yours. Tell me what you know.

I was threatened by him for distributing the poster in London. He claimed to be the copyright owner.

Of the photograph.

Of the photograph. But he wasn't.

No he wasn't. But he threatened you, and you had made a posterised colour interpretation? And he saw this as an infringement to his own interest in the photo?

Yes, I was over in London trying to find distributors for my posters. There was a magazine called *Oz*, that was eventually banned by the British authorities and there was the company called Big O. They were the best and biggest poster company of their time. This is the summer of 1968 and they had a lot of really radical work in their range. I wanted my work included in their range, and they said, we are already taking on the photo version and Feltrinelli has the copyright. I said, no he doesn't, the photographer does. So they took me on and he called and threatened to sue me and to kill me. I said,

'Do I have a choice, can I take my pick?' He said, 'Every man has a choice'. I chose Death, it's cheaper.

The photographer, Alberto Diaz Gutierrez (Korda), was the top Cuban chronicler of the revolution and Castro's personal photographer in a way.

Feltrinelli stole the photo from him, this was reported in a Dutch underground magazine, but now I think the story is, Korda gave him the photo but never expected it to be used or his name obliterated.

Either way, Feltrinelli had walked into his studio in Havana, got the photo and distributed it widely with enormous success. Korda never received any royalties.

He couldn't.

No he couldn't, for many reasons, and there are many people offering commentary at the moment of what those reasons could have been. Some say he was grateful to Feltrinelli as well, for making the image known in the name of the cause. But the bottom line is, he was not really in a position to seek royalties. Castro considered intellectual property 'capitalist bullshit' and Cuba was not a signatory to the Berne Convention on intellectual property at the time, so he was not in a position to even ask. But then almost simultaneously, you were doing the poster. Both the photograph and the poster were under the same publishing house in the UK, did you get any royalties out of that?

No, to be honest they only took a small number and I never got paid by any of these people. I just kept producing the posters, I was enjoying it. And I was feeling that… I know that sounds crazy, but I was feeling that here was this Irish Argentinean that only people like myself would know about, that started to appear in all the shops, and then I started seeing all the variations…

Wait, Che Guevara was Irish?

Yes, he told me this, and I followed it up. I can give you the genealogy. It was Isabel Lynch from Galway, his father's grandmother. So he was third generation Irish.

And so you identified with him as an Irishman?

Absolutely, yeah. And I'll give you a laugh too. Two of my heroes at the time were Che Guevara and John F. Kennedy, poles apart in the Cuban Missile Crisis. The two of them almost brought the world to an end, you know. Not long after, Bobby Kennedy was murdered too, and I later did a different poster of him as well. He was standing up against the Vietnam War and became one of my heroes. I've often thought of making more people in the style of the Che Guevara, but somehow after I had created it, I felt that that was a final and shouldn't be applied to other people. Right now there is a comedian called Ricky Gervais, who uses the exactly same pose as Che on the cover of his CD and all his ads. He's a fat guy with a sort of rubber nose. It doesn't bother me, he's a very good comedian otherwise, but I don't find that it adds anything. Over the years, I have seen so many pastiches of the image, applied to so many other people.

They don't bother you, you find them more to be silly gestures because they don't

have the same strength as the Che image originally had?

Indeed, a couple of years ago, a church in England ran Che Guevara as Jesus, Jesus drawn in the same style that I had given Che, if you can imagine?

Jesus as Che!?

Yes, I mean, it is a very simple style. I had been doing that style long before I did Che Guevara, simply because I wasn't a very good artist. When I was 15 or 16 I would trace an Elvis Presley or whomever from a magazine. By now the image has been used for many causes, many of them worthy, a lot of them very unworthy. There was one variation that I particularly liked, a black image, and in the front of it a green and red vibrating off each other. Very cleverly done, and then Paul Davis, an American artist did a cover for *Evergreen* magazine. And that itself became a great poster. There were Cuban versions of that poster as well, there was an exhibition of Latin American art in Dublin and there on the wall I saw this wonderful Che Guevara poster. But they used his face as part of the shape of Latin America.

Yes, I can see that happening. So you were seeing all these variations coming out of the photograph or out of your posterised version?

Out of my posterised version. Another one was my poster but rendered in 'real life', Che Guevara painted in flesh. Now, to take you fast forward, in the Saatchi gallery, you know the Saatchi collection?

Yeah.

It's all British Sensationalist art. Like Damien Hirst, you know that sort of stuff.

Yeah.

Shark, et cetera.

Absolutely.

There is an artist called Gavin Turk, heard of him?

Yep.

He has done my image, in other words, my version of that image, black on red, on canvas, it's in the Saatchi collection and its worth a couple of hundred grand, which I think is quite funny as well.

And what about Andy Warhol, I've seen his version attributed to your design.

Well, Warhol did his own version. At that stage, everybody knew that image.

Why do you say he did his own thing, I thought he used your silk-screen version?

Yes, but he did his own take on it. You know the way he puts a bluish pastel shadow all around everything. Well he probably drew it in black pastel and then it was printed, the one I saw was bluish. But he wouldn't have been aware of me, he'd been aware of the image.

It seems like the influence keeps going in and out of oblivion at various times. You didn't know Korda, Warhol didn't know you, Feltrinelli thought he knew it all. This was before Google though, so not everybody could know everything at once.

Nobody knew anything. I used to say to people, 'I did that', and nobody believed me.

So what can you say of influence as such, of borrowing elements of existing culture? As an artist, you draw on things you see. You need that to process culture and you take influence in order to push an idea or comment. Do you think culture could exist at all if this wasn't a fact?

I think all artists are magpies, everyone of us. My Celtic work for example, it started off with Mucha and now it's recognisably mine, but you have to start somewhere. At the time I did the Che Guevara poster, I was absolutely absorbed by Polish poster art. They had some amazing graphics coming out of there. And then there were the San Francisco Bay artists. They all produced these extraordinary posters, it was a massive boom. It was the same thing over here, but there was no poster boom in Ireland, so I joined in on the English end of things. That explosion of Carnaby Street, 'Swinging London'.

So the influence issue is at the core of creation. But what is interesting to me about the influence in the Che Guevara poster lineage, is that you can almost draw a straight line of political intent going from Che himself, then Korda's portrait of him that he let go of, and then your poster, all serving 'the cause'. But after this, it kind of explodes into all these contradictory uses. I see myself being at the end of the food chain. I was born in 1967 and my generation is mostly associated with apathy and the death of any revolution!

(laughs)

But I have to say, I've still had a great visual love for this kind of stuff. And the reason I've come to you through this, is that I have had this poster up on my own wall in New York for the last few years, with a stuck on Concorde flying above Che's head. That's my contribution to the image. I made it the year that the Concorde was taken out of traffic. As a sad nod to the end of... you know... the end of that kind of beauty and idealism. And those two together, the perfect revolutionary man and the perfect plane, fading off in memory together. So this is the image we are using for this invite of this show now, but I would say 75% is physically your original poster still, and that's why I wanted to dig into the history of you having made it.

Well it starts with me meeting Che Guevara.

You've said you met him but have no evidence of it, what were the circumstances of this meeting and why are they doubtful?

I was working in a pub, it was a summer job from school, a priest had gotten me the job. I went to the Franciscan College in Gormanston, they got me a job in a hotel in a place called Kilkee, a little remote town, my mother was from there. I was working in the bar one day and Che walked in!

What year was this?

I think it must have been about 1962. But there was no proof of him ever leaving Shannon airport, just proof that he had landed. Nobody ever even believed that he was in Ireland first. Then a photograph of him taken in Ireland appeared, taken by an Irish photographer, only about ten years ago I think. It's only been in the last recent years that the Che Guevara image has come of interest to the public, in terms of its gestation, how the image evolved.

So he walked into your pub?

He walked into the pub in broad daylight. And he had two people with him, they were burly, curly-haired Cubans. I've read that Korda said he never drank, but my recollection is that he ordered an Irish whiskey. I recognised him immediately because I was fully aware of the Cuban revolution. I knew of the facts, that there was an Irish Diaspora in Argentina. We were taught our history pretty well. We knew the founder of the Argentinean Navy was Admiral Brown. O'Higgins, the liberator of Chile, had a city, 'O'Higgins' named after him. I knew of all these close associations between the Irish and Latin America. The same way we are proud of the Irish in North America, a lot of people, if they knew more, would be proud of the Irish in Latin America, in their fight for freedom. I have a book on one of the very first Irish Conquistadores who is very strongly on the side of the Indians. It was Cornelius O'Crowley, an Irish Conquistador. Not everything is always Black or White. But anyway, the Guevara family originally came from Galway and settled in Argentina, along with a huge number of Irish families from the Mid-West, from Westmeath. They later became, what do they call it? 'Whitelace Irish'. They were the educated and slowly rose to the very top of the Argentinean society. Guevara's father was a doctor. Guevara trained as a surgeon and when I met him, he was the Minister for Finance in Cuba.

And what was your direct interaction with him in the pub?

I was only about sixteen I wasn't expecting to speak with Che Guevara. I asked him vaguely about his roots, because he told me his granny was Irish. His great granny, Isabel, was from Galway, but he told me his ancestors were from Cork. I am pretty sure that's what he said.

Did he seem like he was actually there to look at his ancestral land?

No, not at all. He was curious, more from a revolutionary point of view. He had great admiration for the fact we were the first country to shake of the shackles of empire, we were the first country to start bringing down the British empire, which was the biggest empire in the world, if you remember.

But in that pub, to walk around among people and chat? How was his visit officially presented?

It wasn't an official visit. He was stuck. He was on an overnight flight from Moscow to

Cuba. He touched down at Shannon airport. The Soviet airline had a refuelling base there. It was foggy, so his plane couldn't take off, so I think they took a day off.

The Soviet fuelling station makes it quite reasonable.

Aeroflot had a base in Shannon. We are supposed to be a neutral country. Americans now use Shannon as a stopover for their planes going to Iraq. Both sides would refuel there. It's not the hub that it used to be anymore, planes simply over fly it now, in those days you couldn't. It wasn't a momentous meeting, but as a kid it was fun to say to your friends you had met Che Guevara. And they said, 'Who the fuck is that?'. But the personal experience gave me the impetus, that when he went to Bolivia, I'd follow his escapades.

I wanted to get back to the image as such. You said when you first found it in a magazine, you didn't know about Korda. But today, there is such an explosion of Che trivia, and it didn't take me long to learn, through I don't know how many accounts, about the exact circumstances of the photograph: Havana, 5 March 1960, Korda was covering a memorial rally in Havana for the hundred plus crew members and dock workers who died when the arms cargo ship La Coubre exploded in Havana harbour, a terrorist bombing...

It was blown up by the CIA.

Cuba blamed the anti-revolutionary forces aided by the CIA. At the rally, Castro spoke from a balcony and Che stepped up next to him for a few seconds, enough for Korda to shoot him. He has been described in this moment as ' wild-haired', 'detached', 'visionary', 'with an expression of steely defiance'. That already, the image this man already conjured up in real life, on a purely performative level, that must have been a remarkable image of a revolutionary icon to watch, just waiting to be snapped.

Che was pure theatre, it's an Irish characteristic.

This is so amazing to me now when I am reading about all these layers following the photograph, because it is like the photograph was already a second layer to his personal charisma, and that was art already. Korda titled the photo, *The Heroic Guerrilla* but it wasn't published for another seven years, until Che's death in the Bolivian jungle. So when he then got executed by the same forces he was defying in that posture, it makes the image so much more powerful, almost like a premonition.

The reason there was such an interest in a live photograph of his, is that the Americans were determined to photograph him when he was dead. There was a photo in circulation, I was tempted to use the photo of him dead, he had his eyes open, he looked like Jesus Christ, but I felt it would almost be profane to interfere with that picture.

But this was the image that his executioners wanted the world to see. His hands were cut off, he was laid out for everyone to see, and that image was plastered over the walls in Bolivia as proof of his killing. But instead what took off so intensely was the distribution of the heroic Korda shot. I think this is the understanding now, that his photo, but also the cultural ferment of the time, the rallying masses of the student

revolts and the Vietnam War protesters, who needed and image and wanted Che to 'live!', immortalised him as a martyr of the revolution, as someone who really died for an idea. I can only imagine that your poster design must have amplified these sentiments and distribution many, many times over, as you contributed a whole new layer of sensuality, clarity and power to the photo.

You wouldn't be aware of this because of your age, but the image, was essentially a very rebellious image. It wasn't just the fact that he looked like a risen Christ. Because he certainly did. You say, 'steely determination' in his eyes. But he looked like a hippie. Long hair, that was an insult to authority. We all wore long hair to piss them off. And did we piss them off! I was stopped in the streets in Cork and in Dublin and told to cut my hair off! This was a symbol just as much as the man himself. The hair became a symbol. That has to be taken into consideration as well. Remember too, he was a symbol just as much in Eastern Europe as in the West. And in Eastern Europe, that's where all my stuff disappeared, they disliked him and thought he mocked authorities, just as much as he mocked the authorities here and in England and in America. They disliked the image, for they realised how powerful it was. Could a rally around a communist hero still be anti-communist?

Could you talk more about this?

The image of Che Guevara became a symbol of universal rebellion.

It eclipsed the ideology.

Oh, totally! Absolutely. It started off, I believe where it really started off, in Paris in the 1968 revolution led by 'Danny the Red', Daniel Cohn-Bendit, he was shot but he survived. He was someone I admired greatly as well, but he is someone who started using the image during the street riots in Paris, and then it spread to a group called The Provos in Amsterdam. They were beyond radical. And all of us were really focused around the opposition to the Vietnam War and that became an opposition to our own governments. In France it became an opposition against the leadership of Charles de Gaulle, it became an opposition against the government itself, opposition against the opposition. It became an opposition, for the sake of opposition. The opposition parties weren't voicing these people's anger.

You saw all this happen, and what were you thinking?

I was enormously pleased. I thought the world needed changing. It has changed, not exactly the way I like it, but it has changed a lot in the direction I'd like it to go.

But the wildfire economy of the image, really, really served you and your ideas? You thought it should be applied to all those causes simultaneously?

I let the ideas loose, it didn't belong to me anymore. But obviously if you have those views that I have, no matter where you put it, it will always serve those views. I just came back from Russia, and a Che Guevara T-shirt there today would be just as offensive to authorities now as it was in our time.

Today it seems that the image still holds a lot of ground as a symbol for actual re-

sistance. You say on your website that both FARC in Columbia and the Zapatistas in Mexico are using it.

I am not proud of the FARC, they've killed an Irish kid, Tristan Murray. But the most interesting place is in North America. Eight years ago I was in the ghettos of Los Angeles and saw the Che Guevara images appearing. I saw this band, the Black Eyed Peas, use one of those murals in the background for a video. The single went to number one here and in England.

But if we stick to revolutionary intentions...

But no, hold on, that IS revolutionary! This is Black and Latino America taking a symbol of anti-Americanism and plastering it on the walls of their ghettos, in America.

In a music industry context?

No, I am talking about the ghettos!

OK.

Latino ghettos are covered with the image of Che Guevara, and you go up to Belfast, you'll see the same image. But where I think it matters most, is where it is happening now, and that is in America.

I haven't seen any of that, but I have no relationship with ghettos, so I wouldn't know. But it's pretty much consistent with what you are saying, that the openness of the idea allows for that. But to get to the flip side of all of this, because there is also a really dark side of the openness here. And that is that revolutionary images of the past are also more and more introduced into corporate structures these days. And this is where Korda made a point of his limitations in 2000 by suing Lowe Lintas, the British advertising agency that used the image for a Smirnoff campaign. There is a really distinct moment here where together with the Cuba Solidarity Campaign in London, who helped him to fight this cause, he set the record straight, saying that this is corrupt, that Che never drank, that it is exploitation. He got a settlement and then he donated the money to the Cuban health system, to its childcare. I was wondering, if this committee now, after Korda's death in 2001, is still out there watching out for 'unscrupulous use' of the image. Have you ever been contacted by them?

I called them. I offered them all rights I had to my images, which is essentially Korda's image. But I don't think they ever took it any further, I don't think they were that interested to be honest. I said I was the one who had created the poster and had all the documentation, but I suggested I hand over all the rights to whomever it belongs to and they would be the natural caretaker, but I don't think they knew what I was talking about. Wouldn't it be great if they had the whole lineage of it? I've never made any claims to it at all, I am proud of the fact that I was the person, you might say, who helped generate enormous interest in it, and by extension in Guevara himself and his life.

Well, so here is something really depressing I am going to tell you about. I have a recent article here from an Utne reader that is reporting on recent events that has to

do with the copyright. It's from 2 September, 2004 and they say an Atlanta company, Fashion Victim they're called, that is using Honduras sweatshop labour to produce Che Guevara T-shirts, is now suing a Minneapolis company that has been doing the T-shirts for over two decades. They say that they have legally acquired the North American rights in 2002, from Korda's estate who, I must assume, with good intentions is trying to control the copyright by... simply controlling it. But here is the final twist to the story. What I wanted to ask, where do you fit into this?

I'll tell you where I fit in. They approached me to do the image. I said I didn't have the copyright and wouldn't take royalties. And they agreed all royalties would go to disarm. org. And they would make sure that all royalties would be used to buy and ship medicines to Cuba, to break the US embargo. I have that in writing from Fashion Victim. They then researched it further and got in touch with a company that claimed to represent the Korda family and dealt with them from then on.

It says here that Korda's family sold the copyright to David McWilliams' company, Fashion Victim, that has its T-shirts produced in Honduras.

Slave labour.

Yes. So this is the final twist to the story. And whatever that means, it means that that's the circulation of images. Copyright holders die, their families take over, the world changes and we are facing paradoxes. But what I am interested in, is that the whole industry of the Che imagery, the mass industry of Che paraphernalia now, from mouse pads to ashtrays to T-shirts, is mainly using the silk-screen process, which means they are mainly referring back to your posterised version of the image and not the photograph as such. So your creativity is always going to be part of that whole industry. Where does that leave you?

It leaves me on the outside looking in, where I've always been.

A perfect answer.

This interview first appeared on the back of the poster, produced as a piece of mail art, doubling as the invitation for the exhibition Communism, *curated by Grant Watson at Project Arts Centre in Dublin, January 2005. The lay-out of the original has been slightly amended for the purpose of this book.*

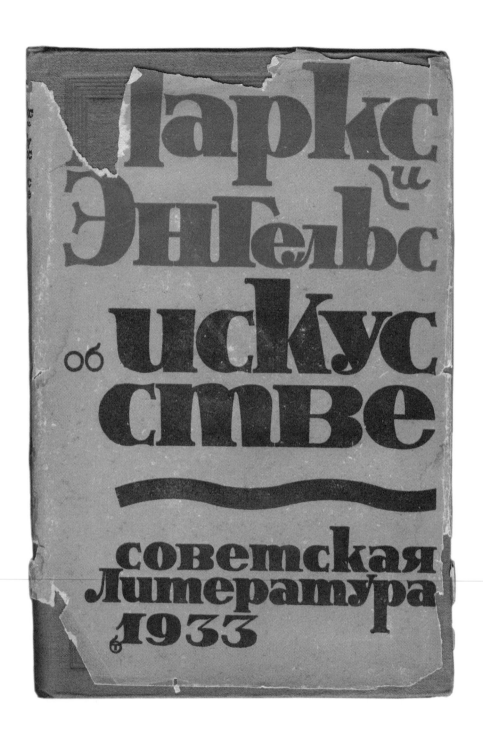

Book cover of
Marx and Engels on
Literature and Art
Moscow 1933

I

'As we know from the *Economic and Philosophic Manuscripts of 1844*, the 'entire move-ment of history [is] communism's actual act of genesis – the birth act of its empirical exis-tence.' Certain periods in this global drama have exclusive value. The 1840s, for example, will always appear as a Copernican revolution in the history of thought, or, to speak with Marx, the earliest manifestation of communism's self-awareness. The form of this mani-festation is so beautiful that it will probably never cease to fascinate and attract.

One of the most profound ideas that Marx articulated in his manuscripts of 1844 never found any further theoretical development in his later texts. As the reader may have guessed, we are talking about what Marx called 'completely crude and thoughtless communism', which appears as private property held in common, and thus is little more than a 'manifestation' of the latter's 'vileness'. This communism 'has not yet grasped the positive essence of private property' and thus 'remains captive to it and infected by it'.

The real course of the material world clarifies the mean-ing of texts that are often inaccessible to immediate understanding. History's arduous movement over one and a half centuries has added a great deal of concrete meaning to these one and a half pages of text. I remember how we read this fragment when I was at school in the late Soviet Union; basically, it seemed like the most accurate possible description of our lives. The communism we knew 'negate[d] the human personality in every sphere'; it appeared as 'the culmination of envy', as 'levelling-down proceeding from the preconceived minimum.' This communism could only think the community as a 'community of labour, and equal wages paid out by communal capital – by the community as the universal capitalist, [...], a regression to the unnatural simplicity of a poor and crude man who has few needs and who has not only failed to go beyond private property, but has not yet even reached it.' This all was not simply theory, but a reality that is difficult to forget even today. (The more famous portions of the *Economic and Philosophic Manuscripts* about alienation seemed far less important to our unseasoned minds back then, even if they made such a great impact on Western contemporaries.)

Of course, there is no law according to which the passage of time brings only clarity. It also works in the opposite direction. Its force seems all the more powerful when it erases meaning and obscures the heart of the matter. Just as Marx's thoughts on crude communism now seem full of real historical content, his definition of genuine communism as the 'positive supercession of private property' (which once had a direct, practical meaning) now sounds like brilliant poetry, appealing to the emotions rather than to the intellect. Communism 'is the genuine resolution of the conflict between man and nature and between man and man – the true resolution of the strife between existence and essence, between objectification and self-confirmation, between freedom and necessity, between the individual and the species. Communism is the riddle of history solved, and it knows itself to be this solution.'[1] Beautiful words that make the spirit soar.

In his introduction to the Italian edition of *The Com-munist Manifesto* published in 1893, Engels wrote of Dante, that he marked both '[t]he close of the feudal Middle Ages, and the opening of the modern capitalist era. [...]' With

Engels, we could repeat that "today, as in 1300, a new historical era is approaching. Will it give us the new Dante, who will mark the hour of its birth?" '[2]

When Engels asked the question, Marx, modernity's Dante, had already been buried at Highgate Cemetery in London for ten years. By now, only fools can deny that he was a literary genius. But our epoch has yet to fully understand the concrete meaning of his work.

II

One possible and necessary movement in this direction lies in the historical study of how Marx's ideas were read and applied in key moments in history, in Lenin's praxis, for example. Another such moment can be found after Lenin's death, in the Soviet 1930s, one of the darkest and most hermetic decades in history, thoroughly mythologised, and fraught with deep contradictions. From the perspective of the problem articulated above, the significance of this time is difficult to overestimate. Never in the history of humanity has the realisation of communism seemed so close; never has its collapse been so tragic. The light this time sheds on Marx's thinking is exclusive in its specific intensity; its theoretical reflections deserve to be saved from oblivion. It seems paramount to find and comment texts that reflect the problems of this epoch, and to bring them to the attention of those who are not indifferent to Marxism. This is how one could sketch out the goal of the Lifshitz Institute, which was founded by a small group of artists and intellectuals from Moscow in the early 1990s.

The prehistory of this initiative's emergence is as follows. In the late 1980s, against the backdrop of massive anti-Communist hysteria, several artists interested in theoretical questions began to pay more and more attention to a strange phenomenon. It suddenly seemed that some texts stood out from the usual senselessness of Soviet dogmatism. The texts in question were written by one of the Soviet authors on aesthetics, Mikhail Lifshitz (1905-1983), notorious as one of the most wooden specimens of Marxist orthodoxy of a Stalinist mould. At first, these deviations from the canon did not seem to be very great. Lifshitz, in a distinctive style that always balanced on the edge of preposterousness, characterised his own relationship to the communist party as follows: 'I have always followed the maxim of St. Cyprian: "There is no salvation outside of the church."' [3] On the one hand, Lifshitz's own texts really do contain a degree of ecclesiastical baggage, stacks of dead formulas, scholastic turns of phrase, or ritual expressions customary to the Soviet epoch. But these stereotypes have undergone a total transfiguration. Lifshitz consciously ignores the fact that certain words have been erased from the Marxist lexicon, and simply continues to use them in their original meaning, sweeping aside the onset of banality with his intonation and the energy of his style.

In other words, the essence of our discovery in the late 1980s was that, putting all outer similarities aside, Lifshitz had very little in common with orthodox Soviet philosophy. His reading of Marx is singular. This impression was overwhelming. Imagine walking through a flea market of cheap paintings, poor reproductions and unconvincing forgeries of classical art. And suddenly, you find a real Chardin. Lying unwanted in the dirt, it costs just as little as all the others. You say: 'This is amazing! It's a Chardin!' But the people at the flea market tell you that this painting has been lying around for fifty years and no one wants to buy it. And anyway, all the other stalls have a Chardin or two as well. And really, it is not all that easy to tell the difference, all the more since the author went to great efforts not to fall out of line, formulating a rigorous credo: 'Wisdom, and not only popular wisdom, teaches that one has to be like everyone else.' Bereft of any garish self-advertisement, Lifshitz's writings speak softly; they count on little more than understanding. As he once noted, 'In our time, there is so much noise that no one pays much attention to theoretical ideas if they are published under names like "Experiments" or "Characterisations."' [4]

Slowly evolving in an extremely hostile environment over the space of several years, the activity of carefully reading and discussing these brilliantly low-key texts was eventually formalised as the Lifshitz Institute, founded in 1994. The two key directions of its work are research and propaganda. The institute's members have collected comprehensive libraries of books and articles by Lifshitz himself, many of which are bibliographical rarities. A significant portion of these texts has been digitised and is now accessible online, albeit only in the Russian language. [5]

Since the project's principal participants are artists, part of their activity also unfolds in the space of artistic exhibitions, where photographs, films, and paintings made in the framework of the project are shown. [6] The Institute also carries out discussions and seminars, sometimes in the format of performances. [7]

The study of the real conditions under which Lifshitz worked plays an especially important role. The goal is to read Lifshitz against the back-drop of the political and artistic debates of the Soviet epoch. Since Lifshitz's birth one hundred years ago, the situation in Russia has changed cardinally not once but several times over. Yet during his lifetime, Lifshitz's basic views remained steadfast. Through his life, he continued to develop idea first formulated in the mid-1920s. What sounded like a call for action in one situation appeared as extreme servility in another, only to re-emerge as a provocation after yet another fundamental historical turn. Of course, a thinker's thought has to stand for itself, but we can never read it without considering the relations of the time. So it is better to consider these relations as fully as possible.

III

Mikhail Lifshitz's biography reflects the fate of Marxism in the Soviet Union. Lifshitz was born in the small Ukrainian town of Melitopol in 1905. At the time of the October Revolution, he is twelve years old. At the age of fifteen, in the midst of civil war, famine, and typhoid fever, he encounters books by Lenin, which make a first deep impression of what philosophy can be. Lifshitz dreams of becoming an artist. In 1922, he travels to Moscow to enrol at VKhUTEMAS, the world's first citadel of proletarian culture, a stronghold of radical innovation. In the mid-1920s, he becomes interested in the dialectics of German philosophy. He studies the German language, and pores over Schelling, Hegel, and Marx, finding his way to a highly independent view of art, which, as he puts it, 'was coloured by the prevalent atmosphere of the renaissance of classical art on the basis of the new social formation that the revolution had created.' [8] He calls this the negation of the dissolution that beset humanity's intellectual values as the old class civilisation met its end.

In 1922, Lifshitz writes his earliest theoretical texts, including *On the Aesthetic Views of Karl Marx* and *Dialectics in the History of Art.* His formulations of the time are infected by avant-garde radicalism, but point in the opposite direction: 'Contrary to the trivial phraseology of our century, absolute beauty exists, as does absolute truth', 'Relativism is dialectics for idiots', or 'The time has come to say farewell to the mousy scrambling of reflection!' It is hardly possible to think of a worse place to assert such ideas than VKhUTEMAS. By proclaiming the return to the classics, Lifshitz draws the consequences of his teachers' central lesson, namely that teachers themselves need to be rejected in full. Further study becomes impossible.

In 1927, Lifshitz makes his fundamental discovery: Marx had his own system of aesthetic conceptions. This is something that no one had suspected. Working meticulously, he begins to collect all of the passages on art in Marx and Engels' writings, eventually publishing them in 1933 as *Marx and Engels on Literature and Art*. This volume has been reissued and translated many times over, often to the credit of other editors, whose alterations damage rather than improve Lifshitz's compilation. In the same year, Lifshitz also first releases *The Philosophy of Art of Karl Marx*, which was later translated into English and published in New York in 1938, and then in London in 1973 and 1976 (with a foreword by Terry Eagleton). This text, written by Lifshitz when he was 28 years old, is the only of his books to find recognition in the English-speaking world. But even those who value his work highly do not suspect that Lifshitz continued his intensive examination of the Marxist view of art for exactly fifty years to come.

The 1930s, and especially their beginning, are the main decade in Lifshitz's life. It is during this period that his main ideas take shape. In 1935, he publishes the book *Questions of Art and Philosophy*, an anthology of his first and ultimately most important texts on the history of social thought. He soon finds himself at the centre of a small circle of like-minded people, who begin to publish the journal *Literaturny kritik* in 1933. This group had a strong influence, especially amongst students. I personally have met old people who voice great surprise when they hear that I am interested in a forgotten philosopher who once was their idol.

In any case, the group around *Literaturny kritik* makes a substantial critical contribution to the literary debates of the time, reflecting the many (often contradictory) voices that emerged to criticise the avant-garde after it ceded its hegemony over culture in 1932.[9] The broader polemic also included the famous Marxist philosopher Georg Lukács, who extended the discussion to the German *émigré* press in the 'Brecht-Lukács debates', held somewhat belatedly in 1936-1938.[10] In 1933, Lukács had emigrated to Moscow, and collaborated closely with the *Literaturny kritik* group in general, and with Lifshitz in particular. However, the widespread idea that Lukács was Lifshitz's mentor seems historically unfounded. Lifshitz's recently published notes show themselves highly critical of Lukács' aesthetic theories;[11] some of Lifshitz's older proponents even claim that it was actually Lifshitz who taught Lukács and not the other way around.

One thing that seems certain, however, is that their literary and artistic tastes converged. Both championed realism over expressionism, naturalism, or formalism, invoking Balzac and Thomas Mann. However, Lifshitz and his closer associates also worked closely with the writer Andrei Platonov, who became one of the journal's most important contributors.[12] Platonov's presence in *Literaturny kritik* and the journal's defence of his work once he fell into disfavour, was one of the reasons that led to the journal's closure in 1941. Too little is known about Lukács' relationship to Platonov to be sure, but it seems difficult to locate the work of the latter within the realist paradigm that the former developed throughout the 1930s-1940s.

In 1937, Stalin's purges accelerate into mass terror. Lifshitz's literary activities come to a complete halt. In 1941, he joins the army and is wounded in combat. He returns to an unrecognisable world. 'After the war', Lifshitz will later remember, 'many things changed. These were not easy times. Upon returning from military service, I felt that I had been completely forgotten. I had reached rock-bottom. Above me, there was an oceanic mass of murky water.'

Stalin dies in 1953. Lifshitz greets the onset of de-Stalinisation and the 'Khrushchev Thaw' with a new article in the journal *Novy Mir* entitled 'The Diary of Marietta Shaginian'. This polemic essay is a cutting satire on the

Mikhail Lifshitz 1945

Mikhail Lifshitz 1920

Discussion of
Lifschitz's article
'The Phenomenology of
the Soup Can' at the
exhibition <u>Pop Art
Classics</u> Stella Art
Gallery, 4 February
2002.

tinsel verbosity of the Stalinist intelligentsia and its astonishing combination of epic exaltation and indifference. It provokes a frenzied response. Lifshitz is officially accused of 'unhealthy, petit bourgeois nihilism' and condemned for 'preaching anti-patriotic conceptions'. Again, he is deprived of any broader readership for years to come.

Fame only descends upon Lifshitz in the mid-1960s, albeit in a scandalous form. In 1966, he publishes a polemic piece against the neo-modernist tendencies in post-Stalinist art with the title 'Why I am No Modernist' in *Literaturnaya gazeta* and follows it up with the book *The Crisis of Ugliness. From Cubism to Pop-Art* in 1968.[13] Both texts subject the entire aesthetic project of twentieth-century art to a scathing critique. Essentially, they develop ideas Lifshitz had already formulated during his time at VKhUTEMAS. He does not only reject the bourgeois world, but also refuses all those hypertrophied forms of protest that Lenin once called 'communism's infantile disorders.'

Most readers had little idea of the role that Lifshitz had played in the 1930s, nor did they necessarily remember his publications from the early 1950s. Thus, his attempts to call the progressive nature of modern art into question falls upon deaf ears; its author is perceived as a living embodiment of half-baked Soviet obscurantism, who had come out of nowhere.

In 1972, Lifshitz publishes the book *Karl Marx. Art and the Social Ideal.* In it, he presents a collection of his work from 1927 to 1967. He is fully aware of the reaction that these texts will provoke in the era of the Soviet intelligentsia's massive rejection of Marxism. In 1973, Lifshitz, who is almost seventy years old and who bears no academic titles, receives the degree of doctor of philosophy for this contribution. Soon afterwards, he receives the title of academician. This late rehabilita-tion earns him the reputation as the most conservative and reactionary writer of the Brezhnev-period, a reputation that persists to this day.

In the last years of his life, Lifshitz works to systematise ideas first voiced in the early 1930s, ideas that did not enjoy any further development due to the dramatic conditions of the time. But in 1983, he passes away unexpectedly. He does not manage to finish many of his undertakings, nor does he live to see the publication of many of the projects he had completed. His huge archive remains in a great number of file-folders (around seven hundred in total). Incidentally, their graphic execution reveals the hand of an artist trained in the school of VKhUTEMAS.

In 1985, Lifshitz's book *In the World of Aesthetics* finally reaches publication. It includes one of his most important theoretical texts, 'A Man of the Thirties'. In the next years, Lifshitz'ss principal works are published in three volumes. The first volume is printed in 1984, the second volume in 1986, and the third volume in 1988. If something seemed amiss during the author's lifetime, then these posthumous publications appear as the apogee of untimeliness. The *perestroika* is in full bloom. The abolition of the entire Soviet system is the order of the day. Other than a small group of enthusiasts, no one pays even the slightest attention to these invaluable contributions to the relation between Marxism and aesthetic philosophy.

IV

At this point, it seems high time to let Lifshitz speak for himself. In a recently published book of rough drafts and notes from the Lifshitz archive, there is a small fragment that reads: 'A common mistake made by many great people – they think that their readers understand not only the *denotatio* but also the *connotatio* of what they are saying, to use medieval terms. Of course, they are also often forced to say something quite different than what is really on their mind, though they still say what they want to say nevertheless. Since many readers and listeners, especially in following generations, know neither the intellectual folklore nor the real relations of the time, they take these words all too literally. Hegel and his ideal of the Prussian police state met this fate, as did Chernyshevsky with his paradoxical simplifications. This is the fate of all of humanity's great conservatives, whose searching, innovative thinking needs to find its expression in a transfigured and even inverted form.

'But if great people simply had to make this mistake, if they are guilty without being at fault, then we ordinary people do not necessarily have to make the same mistakes all over again.' [14]

Of course, this observation can be related back to Lifshitz himself. (In fact, the work of the Lifshitz Institute primarily aims at re-reading his texts against the backdrop of the Soviet era's intellectual folklore and the real relations of this time). But for now, it seems more important to emphasise that this fragment is actually talking about Marx. At risk of formulating the subject of this text too abruptly, we might say that that the 1930s allowed modes of reading Marx that did not take all of his words at face value.

In the 1920s-1930s, *The Communist Manifesto*'s treatment of 'eternal truths' like freedom, justice, religion, and morality was often taken all too literally. Toward the end of the second chapter, Marx and Engels devise the figure of the bourgeois who fears that Communism 'will abolish all eternal truths, instead of constituting them on a new basis, therefore [acting] in contradiction to all past historical experience.' Marx and Engels analyse this fear through the lens of class antagonism, whose fact remains unchanging, though its forms may vary. If class antagonism vanishes, they argue, then so do many 'eternal forms'. 'The Communist revolution', they write, 'is the most radical rupture with traditional property relations; no wonder that its development involved the most radical rupture with traditional ideas. [15]

This sounds like a justification for the total relativisation of all culture as a superstructure that can be annihilated at will, once the Communist revolution is underway. However, when one reconstructs the real situation *The Communist Manifesto* was written in, and the relations that this portion of text was meant to illuminate, it becomes clear that Marx was saying something quite different. The rhetorical 'no wonder' seems to scoff at the unchanging norms of the old world as a polemical device, a paradoxical simplification. But this 'no wonder' can also be read somewhat differently. Have no fear, it seems to say, once the Communist revolution comes, those aspects produced by traditional property relations will already be gone; there is no need to abolish anything. In the light of those texts written no more than four years earlier, this reading sounds far closer to the insistence upon the historical inevitability of genuine communism, and not an apology of crude communism, which in 1844 to Marx was still 'the abstract negation of the entire world of culture and civilisation' by an act of will, and motivated his criticisms of other socialisms and communisms in the *The Communist Manifesto*. However, since this statement against crude communism is cloaked in the rhetoric of political struggle, it now appears in a form easily misunderstood to the contrary.

Under the conditions of quite another political struggle in the 1920s-1930s, it is precisely this special quality of writing that Lifshitz characterises with the words 'great people are often forced to say something quite different than what is really on their minds, though they still say what they want to say nevertheless.' Thus, it becomes all the more important to grasp the inner content of Marx's work, especially since he no longer felt it necessary to explain very often, especially in

Mikhail Lifshitz
after breaking through
enemy lines, 1941

The biographies of
the generation of the
1930s are interrupted
by the war with
fascism. Lifshitz
departs for the
front. He serves in
the Dnepr Flotilla.
The flotilla is de-
feated. In September
1941, he is wounded.
Lifshitz finds
himself surrounded by
the enemy. He spends
September and
October of 1941
slipping through
enemy lines. This
photograph was taken
when he finally made
his way to friendly
troops. His archive
contains the
following note:
'When one officer
was sitting under a
bridge up to his belly
in water as a German
airplane strafed the
road overhead, he saw
a small frog with
little green eyes
and couldn't help but
smile.'

later years. The goal was to uncover this latent vein in Marxism – Lifshitz called it its cultural-anthropological aspect – and to evidence its continuity. Behind Marx's political-economic discoveries about the essence of social formations, Lifshitz saw Marx's philosophy of culture, or – in broader terms – his philosophy of history, which now needed to be exposed in full.

This is exactly why it seemed so important to Lifshitz – from the late 1920s onwards – to study Marx's views on art. In his notes, he writes: 'The main thing is the object of study. A person can only make his contribution, if he has the possibility of resting it upon a special object. My own possibilities were limited in this regard. The only way I was able to realise myself and to say what I had to say was by leaning on the discovery of Marx's aesthetics. I agree that this is not so substantial, though this object cannot be reduced to the method of analysis applied. But why would you want to take my little object away from me? Let me keep it, like a poor dervish's prayer carpet.'[16]

This ragged prayer carpet, which was 'not so substantial', served as the key to unlocking what Lifshitz called the careful rebirth of Marxism's absolute content. 'The genuine classics of Marxism', he writes, 'are hardly unfamiliar with absolute point of view, for which truth, justice, or beauty are not conventions of their time, but are actually the higher meaning of class struggle itself, while genuine value in general belongs to the objective predicates of activity itself.'[17] This was Marx, but Lifshitz was already reading him not only through Hegel, but through Plato.

There was – and seems that there still is – no other way of understanding the meaning of that famous quote from the introduction to the *Grundrisse*, where Marx speaks of 'period of [art's] flowering, […] out of all proportion' with the level of development to be found in society's material base, and point towards the difficulty that the arts of the past 'still afford us artistic pleasure.'[18] Along with the Hegelian conception of the death of art, this quote became central to the Marxist understanding of artistic creativity in the 1930s, in theorists ranging from Benjamin to Lukács, or Max Raphael to Mikhail Lifshitz.

Lifshitz focuses his entire attention on developing a materialist conception of absolute truth (the reflection-theory, to use his terminology). 'In this sense', he writes, 'Marxism's only serious competitor is theology. Everything else looks provisional, incompletely thought out, and shamefully obscured with refined but tasteless phraseology.'[19] In his text 'A Man of the 1930s', basically a short guidebook to the discussions in the Soviet Union at the time, Lifshitz somewhat coyly names one of its sections 'The Truth Exists'. 'The word 'truth', he writes, 'sounds overbearingly loud; whenever I say it, I feel uneasy. But if the reader really finds that I have indulged in any superfluity by using this great word, I ask that he take into account the following mitigating circumstances. The idea of an unconditional truth that is also relative to historical meaning is not as obvious and as accessible in our time as it would seem at first glace. This is why saying it hardly entails breaking down open doors. Quite on the contrary.'[20]

Full of melancholic irony, this last paragraph refers us to the notion of truth that emerged during the 1930s, namely truth as correspondence to the object of understanding. Even the most abstract formulations of those years were determined by the fate of the revolution, and of communism, its social ideal. In his notes, Lifshitz writes: 'Hegel was partially right in asserting that history had ended. He was only wrong to put a period on it too early on, though after all even Marx seems to have been slightly premature with his *Vorgeschichte* or prehistory. The fact is, however, that society either dies or becomes equal to itself, to its notion. In this sense, Hegel is right.'[21]

The only thing Marx was wrong about was the timetable. Not one formation withers away without exhausting the possibilities for development that it contains. In other words, we still have some time for deliberation, which we need to use as effectively as possible, in order to avoid witnessing yet another triumph of private property, first made common through collectivisation and then re-privatised, only gaining new strength in the process.

It seems clear today that the mechanism of the transition from genuine communism to its crude and thoughtless form was set into fatal motion in the 1920s-1930s. Many of this antique tragedy's contemporaries offered deep theoretical reflections on this transition as it was taking place. One of the more straight-forward observations a man of the 1930s was able to make, based upon his own life experience and his reading of Marx, was as follows: under no circumstances will reality ever comply with any of our ideals. But this does not mean that reality does not have its own ideal, which we now need to comply with. (As Lenin put it while taking notes on Hegel's *Logic*, 'the difference of the ideal from the material is also not unconditional, not *überschwenglich*, not inordinate.'[22] In the 1930s, this thought stood as the centre of all debates on art, and not only art).

This is the most general formulation of an exit strategy from the dilemma that humanity continues to face today, as it rapidly comes closer to becoming a unified whole. On the one hand, one sees the fatal arrogance of intellectuals who think that intelligent people can project social forms or economy systems better than the seemingly chaotic interactions of millions of people. In doing so, they fail to understand how much they do not know and in how far the market uses all forms of localised knowledge that each of us are privy to. (Thus, the accusation against communism's arbitrary nature seems misdirected. The critique of conscious-ness' megalomania belongs to the brightest pages of Marxist literature, as something immanent to communism. Reason's rude interventions always provoke a response, as nature, society, and even things wreak their revenge).

On the other hand, there is the fatal arrogance of intellectuals who think that the seemingly chaotic interactions of millions of people, ruled by supply and demand, and doling out bliss and strife with an invisible hand, is the best path of development. Growing more fascinating in its hallucinatory speed day by day, this kind of progress – as we remember from Marx – 'drank, drink, and will drink nectar from the skulls of those who have lost this race for survival'.

To wait for a process – unconscious by definition – to grow more intelligent and to read it lectures on the necessity of doing so, seems naïve at best. But whoever would like to intervene in this process even a little must become more intelligent, so much is clear. The experience of the 1930s showed that even reason – our very own product – can get out of control, ruling us entirely, going against our expectations, rendering our calculations null and void. 'Reason has always existed, though not always in a reasonable form', Marx noted in a letter to Arnold Ruge.[23] Know thyself, moderate thyself, find the real meaning of existence: this is how the wisdom of Marxism was understood in the 1930s.

This might not sound very progressive at all to revolu-tionary ears. At the time, Marx and Lenin were understood as humanity's two greatest conservatives, as people who deeply valued all previous culture and had nothing in common with neopathy. (Lifshitz used this neologism to denote a special type of ailment, the pursuit of anything new.) Of course, the reader will remember Lenin's last article 'Better Fewer, But Better', where he writes, 'We must come to our senses on time and fill ourselves with sound skepticism toward rapid-fire movement forward.' If we strengthen our control over the material forces that rule us, we need to make sure that we do not outstrip the level of control over our own reason, whose origins and developmental tendencies we have yet to comprehend in full.

Conscious forms of consciousness continue to develop, whether the world wants them to or not. Through bitter experience, the birth of communism's empirical being continues, bringing about a perfect form of sociality, equal to its notion, cleansed of egotism. This is precisely why the movement in this direction cannot do without a love for art (which is not unselfish passion, but unselfish passion, as Lifshitz once put it).

Revolutionary action takes place when it stands up against an intolerable force. It is not enough for this force simply to exist. It also has to be acknowledged as something with which there can be no reconciliation. If properly understood, art makes life intolerable under the conditions of total purchase and sale. (Hence, the intriguing theme torture through beauty, developed during the Soviet 1930s). This may be especially true in Russian icon painting, in the painting of Peruggio, or in classical Chinese pen-and-ink drawings, but basically it holds true everywhere: (until it has not become identical to its notion), art is part of the communist movement. It is the most radical critique of reality, the critique of consciousness' erroneous relationship to the world.

The Soviet 1930s witnessed the unfolding of a tragedy on a scale hitherto unknown to world history. In this sense, their status is singular, exclusive. To speak with Hegel, this can only happen once and only with one people. The self-awareness that this epoch produced is invaluable to anyone who remembers that the proletarian revolution constantly criticises itself. With merciless thoroughness, it holds a mockery to the half-measures, weak sides, and ineptness of its first attempts. Learn, learn, and learn, as Lenin put it. The intellectual and artistic experience of those who witnessed the 1930s, embodied in the prose of Platonov, the music of Shostakovich, or the writings of Mikhail Lifshitz, needs to become an inalienable part of communism, understood not as an invented ideal, but as a real movement, overturning the present state of affairs.

Editorial contributions and translation from Russian: David Riff

Dmitry Gutov

Karl Marx, Economic and Philosophic Manuscripts of 1844 Oil, canvas.

50 X 60 cm, 2006

NOTES.
1. Quotes in the preceding section cited after Karl Marx, *Economic & Philosophic Manuscripts of 1844*, MECW, Vol. 3, International Publishers, New York, 1975-2005, pp. 293-295; http://www.marxists.org/archive/marx/works/1844/manuscripts/comm.htm (accessed July 5 2006)

2. Friedrich Engels, *Preface to the Italian Edition of the Communist Manifesto*, 1893, http://www.marxists.org/archive/marx/works/1848/communist-manifesto/preface.htm (accessed July 5 2006)

3. Mikhail Lifshitz, *Chto takoe klassika* [What are Classics?], Iskusstvo XXI vek, Moscow, 2004, p. 105.

4. Ibid, p. 105.

5. These online archives can be found at http://gutov.ru/lifshitz/index.htm and http://mesotes.narod.ru/lifshiz.htm. (accessed July 5 2006)

6. For more on the connection between Lifshitz and its participants' artistic praxis see Dmitri Gutov/David Riff, 'Die Lehre von Marx ist allmächtig, weil sie wahr ist' [The Marxist Doctrine is Omnipotent Because It is True], *Springerin*. Band XI Heft 4 / Band XII Heft 1, Winter 2006, pp. 22-26. English version online at http://www.springerin.at/dyn/heft_inhalt.php?id=45&lang=en (last accessed July 5 2006)

7. For more on the specific mode of these discussions, see Dmitri Gutov/David Riff, 'Complete agreement is the ideal of the human race', *Chto delat/What is to be done?* No. 9, May 2005. http://www.chtodelat.org/index.php?option=content&task

=view&id=201&Itemid=89 (accessed July 5 2006)

8. N.K Gey (ed.), *Kontekts 1987. Literaturno-teoreticheskie issledovania.* [Context 1987. Studies in literary theory.], Nauka, Moscow, 1988, p. 272.

9. For a sampling of the positions of the *Literaturny kritik* group and its associates, see Angel Flores (ed.), *Literature and Marxism: A Controversy by Soviet Critics*, Critics Group, New York, 1938.

10. For insight into the German-language debate, see the excellent volume *Aesthetics and Politics: Theodore Adorno, Walter Benjamin, Ernst Bloch, Bertolt Brecht, Georg Lukacs*, Verso, London & New York, 1977.

11. Mikhail Lifshitz, *Chto takoe klassika*, pp. 99-166.

12. Andrei Platonov (1899-1951) is best known for his novels *Chevengur* (1926) and *The Foundation Pit* (1930). His absurdist, often bizarre portrayals of the realities and utopias of life under the conditions of collectivisation read as an immanent critique of the first five-year plan and have earned him the nickname of the 'Soviet George Orwell'. His work with the Russian language, however, seems closer to Kafka, and, according to his later proponents, prefigures existentialism. Mikhail Lifshitz was one of the first people to recognise Platonov's talent. They remained close friends until Platonov's death.

13. Both have yet to be published in English, but were translated into German by Helmut Barth and published as *Krise des Häßlichen. Vom Kubismus zur Pop Art*, VEB Verlag der Kunst, Dresden, 1972.

14. Mikhail Lifshitz, *Chto takoe klassika*, pp. 106-107.

15. Karl Marx and Friedrich Engels, *The Communist Manifesto*, 1848, http://www.marxists.org/archive/marx/works/1848/communist-manifesto/ch02.htm, (accessed on July 6 2006)

16. Mikhail Lifshitz, *Chto takoe klassika*, p. 158.

17. Ibid.

18. Karl Marx, *Grundrisse: Foundations of the Critique of Political Economy* 1857-1861, Penguin, London, 1973, p. 111, http://www.marxists.org/archive/marx/works/1857/grundrisse/ch01.htm#4 (accessed July 5 2006)

19. Mikhail Lifshitz, *Collected Works in Three Volumes*, Vol. 1, Moscow 1984, p. 45.

20. Mikhail Lifshitz, *V mire estetiki* [In the World of Aesthetics], Moscow, 1985), p. 247.

21. Mikhail Lifshitz, *Chto takoe klassika*, pp. 142-143.

22. Vladimir Lenin, 'Annotations on Book I (Being) of Hegel's Science of Logic', *Collected Works*, Progress Publishers, Moscow, n.d, http://www.marxists.org/archive/lenin/works/1914/cons-logic/ch01.htm (accessed 5 July 2006).

23. Marx to Ruge, September 1843, *MECW*, Vol 3., International Publishers, New York, 1975-2005, p. 142, http://www.marxists.org/archive/marx/works/1843/letters/43_09.htm (accessed 5 July 2006).

FILE Megazine
Vol. 1, No. 2/3, 1972
Art Official Inc.,
Toronto. Edited and
designed by General
Idea

IS THIS WHERE WE SHOULD BEGIN?
AA Bronson/Dont Rhine

Thursday, 4 May, 2006
The Banff Centre, Banff,
Alberta, Canada

AA Bronson: What is communism, or what is intended by the word communism in this case? Is this a capital C communism; is this Marxism? When I think of the word communism, whole histories come up. And communism as a theory is different than communism as a political history. Maybe it is enough to acknowledge that.

Dont Rhine: I think experientially, from your own experience, you could say there is this thing called communalism and that communalism far precedes any political formulations or theory.

So, for example, this commune that I belonged to in the mid-1960s, in Winnipeg, which also had a free-school, what we called a free-store, and an underground newspaper. The commune itself was a house in which our first principle was that anybody who came to the door would not be turned away. If they wanted to move in, they could. It was a very large house – eight of us, originally, with eight bedrooms – and by the time I moved out one year later there were 65 people living there. The second thing was that we shared a communal meal daily. Originally it was quite organised because there were only eight of us, but as it developed and more layers of people moved in, we would take up a collection once a day, like in the late morning, and then a group of volunteers would go out and buy and steal groceries and, usually, make the meal. And the third principle was that all decisions were made by consensus by whoever was living in the house at the time. Every Monday there was a house meeting where all the issues of the week – and there were increasingly more and more issues as time went on – were discussed and hopefully resolved. So that was an attempt to make a very horizontal and open structure. I don't know to what extent that might be called communism or not. How does that intersect with the idea of communism? It's not really about labour, although we had our own store. But that school-store-underground paper thing was kept aside from the house and was run by the original group of eight.

The Artist began to read aloud: 'The history of all hitherto existing society is the history of class struggles.' He put the book down, and turned to his interlocutor on the other side of the room. 'Is this where we should begin?'
The room exhibited all the anonymities of any hotel room: inflated floral patterns on the bedding, one wall painted olive green to offset the beige of the other walls. On the wall alongside the bed, there hung a polite abstraction whose separate wall card offered the only indication that the accommodations existed on the campus of an arts institution. Outside the open glass balcony doors, voices and ornithic life enunciated the afternoon. It was to this hotel, perched on the nape of Tunnel Mountain, that AA Bronson, the Artist, and his Interlocutor, Dont Rhine, had come to think over the subject of communism. Far above the tinsel daily life of New York for the Artist and of Los Angeles for the Interlocutor, the mountains offered a pinnacle for speculative reflection.

And in this commune there was no hierarchy of who was in authority?

No, there were no elected anythings. There did tend to be two or three people who facilitated the meetings. And the original eight had the authority of being the original eight, having found the house, put the whole project together, and developed the idea. But it wasn't a designated authority. It was implicit in their history.

And that authority was granted to them by everyone who was living in the house?

Yes, to varying degrees. I think towards the end, when it got really ludicrously large, then a certain percentage of the people who had moved in had no idea who the original ones were. It became more anarchic, in a bad way rather than in a good way. There were increasingly people who were there to take advantage of it, to get out of it what they could and then move on. The openness started to become a problem. Rules needed to be put in place to give it some sort of structure so it could actually survive. But, in fact, it didn't survive, it closed down. It was extremely idealistic as a project. There was also a point at which we were considering removing all the doors. We even talked about eliminating private property, but that didn't go down very well.

What about sexuality?

It was quite sexually free and experimental. But some of the people in the house were fairly conventional in terms of how they dealt with sex. They kept their sex life private from the rest of the house. And that's, in the end, I think, why the doors did not come off the rooms, because of sex more than anything, sex and bathrooms. There was a group of us at one end of the house that tried to be more open about all that. I never closed my door. There were two or three bathrooms, and the group of us that used one particular bathroom tended to leave the bathroom door open or to use it collectively. One person might be on the toilet while another person was having a bath. We tried to be more open about it. We experimented with group therapy, too. There was a psychologist from Regina who was doing work specifically around the idea of intentional communities. He started coming and doing group therapy with us once a month. I took to that like a duck to water, so he invited me to join him and travel across Western Canada doing workshops with different co-operative groups.

With deer grazing along the roadside below and mountain peaks thrusting their crowns into a sky immune to spring thaw, this site offered the proverbial mountain top. And as migrants massed in New York and Los Angeles in the millions and all of the United States poised on the brink of descent into a Chai Latte Fascism, the Artist and his Interlocutor installed themselves away in their hotel room; surrounded by books with yellowed pages, ghosts, test pattern memories and the urgencies storming a nation away.

'Perhaps we should begin earlier.' Mused the Interlocutor, distracted by the soundscape blowing in through the opened sliding doors. 'A spectre is haunting ~~Europe~~ [the world] – the spectre of ~~Communism~~ [public gay sex]. All the Powers of ~~old Europe~~ [the world] have entered into a holy alliance to exorcise this spectre: Pope and ~~Czar~~ [President], ~~Metternich~~ [Evangelist] and ~~Guizot~~ [Imam], ~~French Radicals~~ public decency homosexuals and ~~German~~ police spies.' 'I took some liberties with the original.'

'Aren't we obliged to?'

Only in community [with others has each] individual the means

Would this have been considered Gestalt therapy?

Fritz Perls' first book had come out and he had established the Gestalt Institute on Vancouver Island just that year, I think. So it was definitely influenced by Fritz Perls' writings but it was not explicitly Gestalt. But it was similar in the sense that it all started from the practice that what we have in this room here and now is us, relating to each other. And that's all we're going to talk about. We're not going to talk about anything that happened in the past, anything that will happen in the future, we're only talking about the present moment in this room with these people and nothing else. So in that sense it was very much like Gestalt. I travelled with him across Western Canada, ending up at Simon Fraser University. We also had one very interesting session with members of the Gestalt Institute. They had heard about his work and invited him to join them in a professional therapy group. It was him and me together with three or four people, not Fritz Perls himself, but three of four people from the Institute. And we did a sort of session amongst ourselves, which I found horrendous. I hated it. Hated it. Simon Fraser was fine but this session with the Gestalt people was hell.

And why, because it was so dogmatic in its language?

My mentor's idea was that you're never invasive. You take people up to their blocks, hold them there, and let them see and experience the block as a block. You never push them through. You never put anybody into crisis. You bring them up to a point just before the crisis. It has to be very carefully done. But with the Gestalt people, they seemed extremely aggressive comparatively – really eager to push people, to point out your blocks to you, plummet you through them without knowing whether you had the capacity to deal it with or not. They were very harsh with me. Thinking back on it, I think it was actually homophobia. That's what I think – a bunch of straight guys and one little gay boy. I was the vulnerable one: I was younger than all of them. I had no training. They were all trained. I only had this training from the psychologist I was travelling with. It was all sort of intuitive on my part. This one therapist in particular attacked me quite viciously. After that session, I stopped doing therapy groups all together. I just left it all behind. But at any rate, I had gained all those skills – group facilitation skills and bringing people together.

of cultivating his gifts in all directions; only in the community, therefore, is personal freedom possible. In the previous substitutes for the community, in the State, etc. personal freedom has existed only for the individuals who developed within the relationships of the ruling class, and only insofar as they were individuals of this class. The illusory community, [...] since it was the combination of one class over against another, [was] not only a completely illusory community, but a new fetter as well. In a real community the individuals obtain their freedom in and through their association.
Karl Marx, *The German Ideology*, ed. C.J. Arthur, ElecBook, London, 1998, pp.118-119

'You once described your current solo work as being very un-ironic. What obviously comes to my mind is the shift in your own biography in terms of transitioning from working in a collective situation to working in a personal situation.'

The Artist leaned back in his chair. A certain degree of automatism captured his voice. It was a subject that permeated any reflection on the past; a subject that

When you arrived in Toronto were you seeking an analogous experience?

That's the reason I moved to Toronto. I knew a group who had founded a place called Rochdale College, which was affiliated with the University of Toronto. Rochdale College was an experiment in having a very horizontal living and teaching cooperative situation on a large scale. They started with two big old houses adjacent to each other, and in the garage behind them the Coach House Press, which was an early alternative press. A rather wealthy young man got involved whose father was a developer and he knew how to make things happen. They actually managed to build a fourteen storey high-rise that was designed to have a variety of kinds of living experiments within it. The unfortunate thing was that in order to raise the money they had to design it so it could be used as an old folks' home if it failed. It had commercial spaces on the ground floor, teaching spaces and office spaces on a couple of floors and then above that each floor was divided into two parts. One wing was more or less a conventional university set-up with rooms lined up along a hallway; the other was an *ashram* made up of about ten rooms around an open common space with a shared kitchen and shared bathroom. One of the *ashrams* was occupied by a witch's coven, another was a yoga-based vegetarian group, and so on. One whole floor was a group devoted to ceremonial magic. There were twelve floors of that. And on the top floor there were more conventional apartments, like two bedroom apartments, mostly occupied by the original founders.

And this is where you stayed?

I moved there because friends of mine had just opened Rochdale and I wanted to see it. Everybody was talking about it. I went and they made it possible for me to live there for free, sharing a room with Mimi, who I knew from Winnipeg, and who was later instrumental in bringing General Idea together. I lived there several months before I had to move along. And I got very involved with the place. I apprenticed at the Coach House Press, which produced all sorts of visual and written paraphernalia for Rochdale, like their calendar, a publication so layered in images and colours that it was impossible to read, and a little experimental magazine called *Image Nation*. And people like Allen Ginsberg came through for the teaching. The College was very poetry-based because of Coach House Press.

cast any recollection in an ambivalent relation to the present. 'With the deaths of Jorge and Felix I found myself thrown into being very much alone. I think because of the uniqueness of our situation and the communication between us there was no way, highly unlikely, that I'll ever be able to develop that again – it happened through a very unique sequence of events at a particular point in history when things were happening very fast. I find myself feeling very alone in every way. Sometimes I feel that I should allow myself to incorporate a more ironic language again, but I don't know quite how to do it. Maybe it can only happen, for me, in a more collaborative setting. It's funny, I have a whole heap of people that I've been supposedly doing collaborations with, yourself included, that have never quite come to fruition. There're all these collaborations that have never happened, some to a lesser or greater degree. With you, we got at least partway along. Most of them, nothing has happened. Three or four years ago, I talked to Michael Elmgreen and Ingar Dragset about doing a collaboration and we've never got any further than that, than saying we want to do a

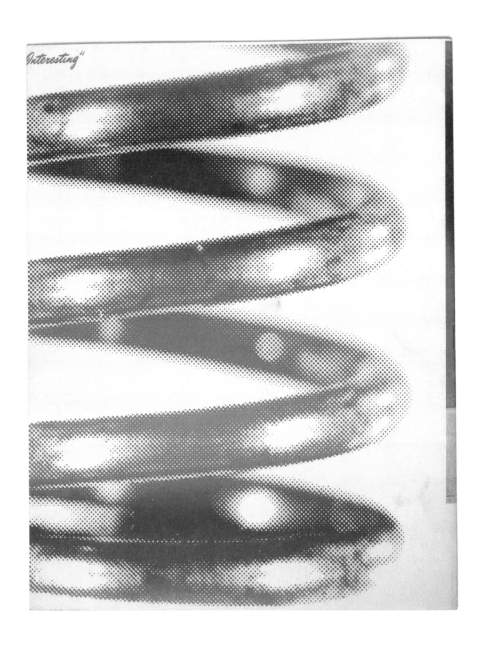

"Interesting"

Image Nation
volume number unknown
Rochdale College,
Toronto, 3 April 1969
design by
Coach House Press
(back cover image)

And there was a theatre troop connected to the building, Theatre Passe Muraille, which I got involved with as a graphic designer. Their first production, *Futz*, opened with the entire cast naked slithering down through the audience, over people's laps and so on. The production was raided by the police and we were all hauled into jail. So that's why I went to Toronto, for that whole experiment which eventually failed and became an old folks' home. Rochdale had some sort of elected structure, I don't quite remember how it worked, it was a co-op essentially. It was all self-governing. Eventually the Hell's Angels took over as the security force, drug dealers flourished, and the place devolved into a series of standoffs with the police that led to it being closed.

How did Rochdale have the capital to sustain itself, or not?

You were supposed to pay rent to be there. There was some sort of sliding scale. And the College rented out space: there was a bookstore, a bank and others on the ground floor. And there was their restaurant. The restaurant was highly experimental. It was on the bizarre side. The menu consisted of long lists of ingredients, and you could ask for anything that could be made from any of those ingredients and it would be made to order. Everybody was so drugged out it didn't matter, but you would order and the food would turn up three hours later. The place was full of hashish and marijuana smoke, and a little monkey was always swinging through the metal superstructure that held the booths. It was really hilarious. The restaurant was an amazing environment visually and socially, it was a great place. So that was my second experiment in communalism.

When you moved into the storefront with General Idea in 1969, did you think about that in your mind as part of a continuing history?

Absolutely. When we moved into the storefront, when General Idea began to form, it was just a bunch of people sharing a house. But it quickly became more, because we were all creative people. We started to do these homemade projects together to entertain ourselves, and eventually it got to the point where we were committed to continuing as a group. At that point I introduced the idea that we should make decisions by consensus. There were basically three of us making decisions; Jorge, Felix and I.

collaboration. There are quite a few people like that.'

'Do you think that has something to do with the fact that none of these collaborations have been part of your everyday life?' The Interlocutor asked, his voice cast in the familiar register that characterised much of the exchange that afternoon.'

'Probably that's a big part of it.' The Artist confessed. 'I'm used to making art out of a daily practice of living together, of being together. To actually go and sit in a studio and work on a project, that way of doing a project, is quite alien to me. I've never really done that. It's always been my life and my work immersed in each other.'

After a moment's pause, the Artist looked up as if awakening from a murky sleep: 'Where does this take us in terms of communism?'

'[C]ommunism is the establishment of a communal life style in which individuality is recognized and truly liberated, not merely opposed to the collective. That's the most important lesson: that the construction of healthy communities begins and ends with unique personal-

And the women who were with you initially had left by this point?

In the first year only Mimi lived with us, in fact it was Mimi who found the house and came up with the idea. After a year, we moved to a much larger space and Granada moved in with us. Mimi and Granada were both very involved in what we did. The consensus involved them as well at that point. There were also a couple of loose people at the edges who would come and go. Pascal, a transgendered ex-opera student with a phenomenal vocal range became part of the troupe for some time. And we realised if we were going to be able to work together we couldn't gang up on each other.

So the group was this core, but then with a little floating, and you introduced from your experiences with previous communal situation the idea of consensus…

… the idea of consensus and the idea of one meal a day together, always. But then we very quickly added morning coffee to that. Morning coffee and dinner were always done as a group. It was actually surprisingly similar to that original commune: There would be the thing of, in the morning over coffee, while opening the daily mail, deciding what we were going to do about the dinner, who was going to cook it and who was going to buy the groceries. It was always organised every morning for the evening. And it was always done in a way that whoever was around could join us.

So you never turned anyone away.

If anybody happened to be there, they would join in the dinner. So there were often ten or twelve people for dinner. We had a big round table, it was often a very large group around that table.

And then money for the food, was the food also bought and stolen?

A little bit was stolen still at that point, sometimes a lot! But it was mostly bought. We took up collections from amongst ourselves. I don't really remember. I suspect we must have at least gone through a period of trying to budget. We were so incredibly poor that I think we just relied on whoever had money at the time.

ity, that the collective potential is realized only when the singular is free. This insight is fundamental to the liberation of work.'
Félix Guattari and Antonio Negri, *Communists Like Us: New Spaces of Liberty, New Lines of Alliance*, trans. Michael Ryan Semiotext[e], New York, 1990, pp. 16-17

'*There's a great formulation in psychoanalysis: demand minus need equals desire,' said the Interlocutor, taking his role in the encounter literally. 'This has made sense to me a lot in relationship to politics. A community constitutes itself around a specific struggle, or a set of struggles. Sometimes you're successful and your needs are met. But then there's this demand to continue and some will say that's just because you've institutionalised yourself. I also think it's because there's an incredible amount of enjoyment that exceeds any demand that that organisation has made. It seems like in some of the practices you've been involved with, especially General Idea, the demand is almost instrumental to the desire and not the other way around.'*

'It was interesting in General Idea to what an extent pleasure was a big part of it. The pleasure of

45

Was there any discussion about division of responsibilities or did that sort of happen organically without having to be discussed? You've talked about the meals, but taking care of the place, paying the bills…

It was very loose. I think I tended to pay the bills, but I have no idea why. But other than that, the place was always a mess. Every now and then we would have these cleaning frenzies. And this second place we lived in was huge, it was two floors of an old office building. It was probably five to six thousand square feet, so all the rooms had names and they were decorated in different ways: the Blue Ball Room, the Jungle Room, and so on. And we had a big studio room where we started *FILE Magazine*. *FILE* was also this communal activity that we dreamt up together and did together. There wasn't really a hierarchy in the early days of *FILE*. It was very much a communal project.

FILE exceeded the people who lived communally? There were more people involved in FILE than lived in the house? Or was it the other way around?

I think at the very beginning everybody in the group was involved in some sort of way, however peripherally. It was just a part of life. Making *FILE* was part of our daily life. There was a woman we hired on a grant programme who became our secretary for a while who was completely inefficient because she had beautiful cursive handwriting. She would write everything out long hand, it took her forever. And we would incorporate stuff by other artists from other cities, other countries. But essentially it came out of that group. And we'd go everywhere together. We had this image in Toronto as being this sort of…

Posse?

… yes, posse. And we would do things to heighten it. We were big thrift shop enthusiasts. We were always out combing the city for cheap stuff of any sort. And we would go on these rampages. There was a period where we were all wearing homemade sweaters with reindeer and snowflakes on them. We would go to parties with all of us wearing reindeer sweaters – or all of us wearing Hawaiian shirts, with platform shoes. We would make appearances. We tried to be outrageous about it.

Can I introduce something into this recollection? In much

working together played a big role in what we decided to do and how we did it. Rather than thinking in more strategic ways about what was going to advance our career (to return to that idea), we tended to think about what would be most … I guess we were trouble-makers. What would be the most questionable activity we could do in a particular situation? We were mischievous in a way, but the mischie-vousness was in a sense a way of questioning. We had the function of jokers – the joker being the only one who can criticise the king.' The Artist punctuated his words with a wicked laughter. His eyes shut tight, his mouth gaping, shaped by benevolent mirth and a vicious delight in what injury could be inflicted on the proverbial monarch.

'The community of interrupted myth, which is commu-nity that in a sense is without community, or communism without community, is our destination. In other words community (or communism) is what we are being called toward, or sent to, as to our ownmost future. But it is not a "to come", it is not a future or fi-nal reality on the verge of fulfillment, pending

FILE Megazine
Vol. 2, No. 3, 1973
Art Official Inc.,
Toronto. Edited and
designed by General
Idea. This was the
special IFEL issue
designed on the
occasion of an
exhibition at the
Musée d'art Moderne
47   de la Ville de Paris

that I'm familiar with in terms of theoretical understandings of communism, there's always this notion that there is a sort of idealism and utopian aspect, but the utopianism is directed as a critique against something. It's directed as a critique against existing forms of exploitation. And obviously there's a whole range of feelings about that: you're angry at people being exploited, you're pissed off at this, or you're feeling melancholic about this loss so you develop a safer space. I'm wondering was there any sense of opposition to something in these experiences?

Opposition is maybe not quite the right word. It's more like we were trying to create a parallel universe. We didn't want to work the way work was constructed in the normal day-to-day world. I don't think we discussed it in analytical or political terms. But it was more like: 'We feel that we can live our lives the way we want to live them, and be creative the way we want to be creative in a communal way. And we, in fact, don't have to participate in the so-called norm in the way that things are structured out there. We don't have to have suburban houses with two-car garages. And if we play our cards right, we can also generate money. We can create a different living/working environment and situation. We can generate capital in a productive way for ourselves and in an adequate way to live without necessarily having to be financially successful.'

You're speaking here specifically of the early General Idea days?

Yeah, we would talk about it quite a bit. I was determined not to have to have a job. We were definitely counter-cultural. It was definitely part of a counter-cultural strategy. One thing, going back to the commune in Winnipeg, one of the eight people who started that commune was an economist who had very sophisticated and developed ideas, from an economist's viewpoint, about what we were doing politically and socially. All of that bled over into what was happening with General Idea. I can't say that we would discuss it in specifically Marxist terms, but the structure of it was very much that. When we first went to Europe, which was in 1976, we were picked up very quickly by the European art scene. Suddenly we were doing a lot in Europe, and the reason was that we were seen as a Marxist group. We were seen, and our work was seen, as being critical. And I guess it was, but …

It was more on an intuitive level than an analytical level?

only the delay imposed by an approach, a maturation, or a conquest. For if this were the case, its reality would be mythic – as would be the feasibility of its idea.'
Jean-Luc Nancy, *The Inoperative Community*, trans. Peter Connor, et al. University of Minnesota Press, Minneapolis, 1991, p. 71

Risking a suffocation on the free association of his colleague, the Interlocutor ventured into speculation. 'Communal life came out of larger developments within the culture that were you were talking about, around specific ideas and around specific critiques. Certain old ways of living were no longer seen as valid. Does that sort of cultural ferment that can sustain experiments and new forms of living, does that exist? Or where does it exist?'

'Where does it exist?' The Artist asked, his voice scored with lament and longing. 'There are, for example, the radical faeries and the loose communal structures that come out of that movement. It's funny, but I find that I have absolutely no interest in it. Within the art world right now, there's suddenly a big interest in collaboratives, or whatever they call them. Is that what they call them? It's difficult to make

To some degree it was more on an intuitive level. For example, we did all these self-portraits of Jorge, Felix and I: the *Men Working* series. It was in a way about labour. By then, the others had moved on and there were only the three of us. We went through all these post-war images, especially from *FORTUNE* magazine. *FORTUNE* is a wonderful repository of images of men working together, of the fact that it is men who do work, and then that they work together. And in the advertising we found countless images of three men: three architects, three construction workers, three men pouring over plans, making decisions. It's all about making decisions. So we did a lot of photographic pieces that were, in a way, reproductions of those poses but with us as models, together with found images of a similar nature. Those works were picked up and exhibited a lot. As the word got out that our work could be seen from this more theoretical viewpoint, then people in North America – well, in Canada anyway, I don't think the Americans ever caught on to it – but in Canada that enlarged people's vision of what we were doing. Until then they just thought of us as some sort of weird campy… they didn't know what. They didn't know what to make of us – silly, some sort of silly thing.

And were you collectively, individually, reading? What were you reading?

There's a catalogue of early General Idea, *Search for the Spirit*, that has an article by me called 'General Idea's Bookshelf.' It's a text about what we were reading through the years 1969 to 1975. There are several streams of reading: for example William Burroughs, as well as some Gertrude Stein, and other typical lesbians-between-the-wars. From the William Burroughs standpoint, the really interesting thing is his idea about images as viruses that we picked up and ran with for the rest of our careers. And ideas about the world of corporate culture which are embedded in his writings, a viewpoint of corporate culture and of how images are used as viruses, the sort of Big-Brother idea of the world. The world out there is something we didn't want to be involved with and that's how we saw it, that was how Burroughs saw it. We were also reading a lot of anthropology in the early years, especially Claude Lévi-Straus, and then taking those theories and trying to apply them to North American society. We had an anthropological view of our own society. Dinner would often turn into a huge discussion around whatever we were reading. We read

out what it's about, really. Whether real or another form of marketing.'

The Interlocutor speculated aloud, 'The other place where it still exists completely outside of the art world – totally outside of the art world – is in communes that have a sort of social mandate. Jonathan House or even Camp Sister Spirit – different situations where you have people living communally because of a religious or social commitment they have taken for a preferential option for the poor. The art world is anathema to this. Or is it?'

'The art world,' grumbled the Artist, 'certainly in New York, is entirely about the market place. I do not find it life-sustaining. It's not interesting for me. It doesn't give very much. It's mostly about creating collectables for rich folk. And yet, there I am. I find myself quite attracted to religious community because of that. Although, I don't know what religious community, I don't see anywhere where I fit in. I'm constantly thinking, maybe I should go to seminary. Maybe I should go and study something. Wanting some sort of life within which the idea of vocation, for example, is a baseline when the whole idea of vocation a lot of Roland Barthes, the other French structuralists too, but especially Barthes when his books first appeared in English, which was, I'm guessing around 1973. We got totally into all of that, especially the book *Mythologies*. We also read *Système de la Mode* in French – we loved anything to do with fashion!

Did you know about his sexuality?

No, not at all. The *Society of the Spectacle* was a major text for us, and also because in my underground newspaper days, the Situationist International had a cartoon strip… you know, all the underground papers were connected. We were all sending each other things all the time, so we would get stuff from the Situationist International all the time in Winnipeg.

What did you think of their inescapable critique of capitalism? Did it reinforce what you had intuitively felt and understood?

We were totally with it. We were totally energised by it. So things like the Miss General Idea Pageants that we did were, in our minds, completely in alignment with the critique of this kind of media spectacle. Those are the sorts of things we were reading in the early to mid 1970s.

Were you aware much of anarchist theory and history?

A little bit. Canada has always been a major centre for anarchism. George Woodcock was one of the major anarchist theorists, lived in Ontario somewhere.

And you were familiar with him?

That time from the mid-1960s to the mid-1970s there was so much ferment. There were so many ideas being thrown around that it was impossible not to pick up all these things even if they were in second or third hand form, in Winnipeg especially, because Winnipeg was, in fact, the centre for communist thought in Canada. There was a communist bookstore that was very influential.

Was it Trotskyite?

I'm not actually quite sure. There were labour riots in Winnipeg in the teens. Winni-

seems to have vanished from the art world, or at least the art world that I'm part of.'

'Truth to tell, the best weapon against myth is perhaps to mythify it in its turn, and to produce an artificial myth: and this reconstituted myth will in fact be a mythology. Since myth robs language of something, why not rob myth?'
Roland Barthes, *Mythologies*, trans. Annette Lavers, Jonathan Cape, London, 1972, p.135. Cited in AA Bronson, 'General Idea's Bookshelf, 1967 - 1975,' in *The Search for the Spirit, General Idea 1968 - 1975*, ed. Fern Bayer, Art Gallery of Ontario, Toronto, 1997, p. 20

'I just do not know what to do with that word,' the Artist said. 'It is too filled with meaning. Its historical connotations come too quickly to mind to make the term useable for us. It is not debased, degraded, or empty enough to use. It has not been co-opted enough by capitalism and the very forces against which it stood in opposition.'

His Interlocutor searched the mountainous vista for a solution to the impasse. 'Perhaps we could accelerate its debase-

peg was a centre for communist intellectual thought, not so much capital C communism, but small C communism. But also, having two universities, it was very much an intellectual centre. Plus it was a big centre for Jewish intellectuals. There were a couple of radical Rabbis who were noted at the time, although I don't remember their names. We were all reading Martin Buber back then, and all that stuff, during my commune days. Felix was in Winnipeg at the same time, Mimi too, we were all part of the same scene. There was a gallery across the street from our free-school and store, an art gallery and a head shop combined, where Felix had his first exhibition. We were intimately connected with each other.

Can I pose something to you? Do you think that since there was this general climate of these ideas, that these ideas were not off here to the side, that they were really permeating the culture, that in some respects the projects that you were involved in accepted all of those critiques and those ideas as given? What you were interested in was the actual lived experience of those ideas?

Yeah, that's probably not one hundred per cent true, but certainly that could be said about us. We were swimming in the theories of the moment. The fact that we were constantly reading books and having these discussions around this round table would suggest there was another layer to it. It wasn't just that, but the experiential part of it was the most important part. How are we living our lives, and how are we going to live our lives? How are we going to get to the end of our lives without having to succumb to participating in that corporate and/or capitalist culture? Even in relation to the art world, how can we not relate to the art world in the traditional way with collectors and galleries and all that stuff? How can we situate ourselves so that we can fall outside of that and be more independent?

But so many of the experiments that came out of that moment would not have shared your embrace of silliness and ecstatic enjoyment and celebration.

No, absolutely not. The Cockettes, maybe, and Charles Ludlam's Theater of the Ridiculous, both of which we were familiar with. No, that's very true. In fact, the psychologist who I had worked with in Winnipeg, I told him about General Idea, and he came to visit. And he was very disapproving of the whole thing. He felt it was too unconscious. I think the degree of camp going on, of which there was a lot, it

ment. Perhaps this should be our collaboration: to appropriate the term for a series of projects that hollow out the term communism.'

Reclining on the bed, like an analysand, the Artist burst excitely: 'A sex club named "Communism".'

The Interlocutor rose, pulled to his feet by the possibility of a polyamorous relational art. He scanned the mountains for entrusted features to such a proposition. 'A hole in the floor into which people could piss, shit or cum, degrading the very foundations of communism. Perhaps we should propose an exhibition for the Museum of the Revolution where visitors take part in a collective humiliation and degradation. Speeding along the emptying of the term so it can finally have some valence again.'

It was as if clothing the idea in flesh knocked the wind from the room. The Artist dissolved into the flat surface of the bed. 'It is still too filled with meaning.' He sighed. 'A project like that would just be seen as transgressive and not mischievous.'

Heeding this cautionary reasoning, the Interlocutor turned his back on the window. The mountains would reveal nothing of was extremely arch, the whole thing was an extremely witty environment, so rather than questioning ourselves as to what we were saying when we said something we totally went into the campiness of it. We allowed ourselves free rein. He pulled me aside and said, 'How can you be doing this after the work we did together?' He wanted something more earnest, I guess. I remember just feeling disappointment that he didn't get it. But I also realised at that point that probably most people didn't get it. People saw us as somehow akin to Andy Warhol's factory, which we weren't really, except for some overlay of glamour. But in our case it was fake glamour. We weren't serious about glamour. We didn't really think we were glamorous. It was like a parody of glamour. So it was quite different. More like Jack Smith, although we weren't aware of him at the time.

It seems also with the Factory versus the work that you were doing, there was a very different relationship to cultural aspiration.

Warhol had a career, he was a businessman first. We did not have careers; we had vocations, not careers. We were adamant about that. That was really a central idea: being artists was our vocation, it wasn't a choice, it was just what we were. And we were trying to live it as a vocation and not a career. Nowadays, when all these art schools are beginning to have career training and courses where you learn how to have a career, I always feel very… it sends a shiver through me, that idea of training people to have careers.

It's the revenge of the FORTUNE *magazine, that now we can talk about art as a profession.*

communism. Collaboration would end, like it began, in an ephemeral encounter.

'It is now possible to complete the semiological definition of myth in a bourgeois society: myth is depoliticized speech. One must naturally understand political in its deeper meaning, as describing the whole of human relations in their real, social structure, in their power of making the world; one must above all give an active value to the prefix de-: here it represents an operational movement, it permanently embodies a defaulting.' Roland Barthes, *Mythologies*, trans. Annette Lavers Jonathan Cape, London, 1972, p. 143

Loving Couch Press
Vol. 1, No. 9
Winnipeg, Canada,
undated (circa 1968)
cover image of Yoko
Ono. Design by AA
53   Bronson

(Above, Top) Cornelius Cardew at the anti-fascist concert 'They Shall Not Pass!', 5 December 1981. The concert was organised in a community hall in Camden Town, London, to commemorate the 45th anniversary of the Battle of Cable Street and the Spanish Civil War

(Above, bottom) Cornelius Cardew constructing Scratch Cottage at Alexandra Palace, 1971. Luke Fowler, <u>Pilgrimage From Scattered Points</u> 2006, digital reprint of a photograph by Alec Hill, C Type print

MINERAL FUTURES
Rob Stone

'The dealer in minerals sees only the commercial value but not the beauty and the specific character of the mineral: he has no mineralogical sense'.
Karl Marx
Economic and Philosophical Manuscripts of 1844

'A careful Florentine craftsman divided the stone I am now thinking of – the portrait stone – into thin layers so as to be able to be able to follow the changes in the markings. Just once the saw went through the right place. Just once it revealed on either side the phantom portrait which had been hidden for thousands of years and which is only a portrait, or even a sign, if the beholder collaborates. Before and after it is but an indistinct image in the process of becoming another image, another portrait, or a hallucination of palaces, ferns, birds and Lilliputians'.
Roger Caillois
The Writing of Stones

The Stones Chorus

An unblinking malice of almost mineral character haunts two musical moments. Grumpy was the very epitome of unreasonable bolshevism. When he was required to join in the dwarves' rendition of the *Silly Song* for Snow White, he turned a stare on her. But not just on her. He turned that gaze on his peers and on the calliope at which he was expected to perform. He was an adept musical improviser, and his mineral balefulness is audible too. It is in the discordant blare he conjured to prod the reticent Bashful into voice. Bashful sang (of a purposeless encounter with a mad polecat). Then, to Grumpy's accompaniment, they all sang, in chorus:

'Ho hum, the tune is dumb
The words don't mean a thing
Isn't this a silly song
For anyone to sing?'

Though mean, and sometimes sentimental and sometimes timid, Grumpy never became a hospitable or accommodating figure. He never really warmed to Snow White. He never warmed to her nor to the imperial project of urban renewal towards which she directed her woodland friends, and to which he became himself subject. Given his circumstances, his skills and sensitivities, there was no reason why he should have. Even according to Marx's very earliest definitions, Grumpy was pathologically alienated and self-alienated – and knew it.

This is one musical moment. The other is that when experimental composer, Cornelius Cardew, turned a chill glare on Ezra Pound. Ideological leanings in Pound's translation of Confucius's ethical work, *The Great Learning*, had come to trouble him. Already Cardew had used the first paragraphs of Pound's interpretation of *The Great Learning* as a basis for one of his own monumental works. 'Paragraph 1' of Cardew's own interpretation of *The Great Learning* has become a kind of institution: a familiar and much-loved treasure in the canon of experimental works that were produced in Britain during the 1970s. It too involves a chorus. It is recited though, rather than sung:

> 'The Great Learning takes root in clarifying the way wherein the intelligence increases through the process of looking straight into one's own heart and acting on the result; it is rooted in watching with affection the way people grow, it is rooted in coming to rest, being at ease in perfect equity.'

This collective recitation is also accompanied, but not in the sense that the chorus of the *Silly Song* is contained and marshalled by a ditty. It accompanies itself. The words of each speaker are lent fleeting counterpoint by the syntaxes and idiolects of their fellow performers as they work their way through the text; exploring its textures and those produced by the concerted voices of others. There is no tune to follow, not even metre; not as such. Or rather, such imposed regularity as may be suggested by the text is surpassed. Its outlines are burst by timbres and syncopations, as words patter and fall. Often these leaking extraneities may lead to a performance of the work sounding amateurish, or under-rehearsed. This would be the locus of an aesthetic and political virtue. Cardew's profound disappointment with the sentiments conveyed by Pound's words led him to think them decadent, and worse, totalitarian. Yet, he continued to allow the performance of 'Paragraph 1' of *The Great Learning*; even if only as an object lesson in the public mechanics of self-criticism.

In these two instants, both Grumpy and Cardew found themselves caught at thresholds of personal and political renewal. Each is brilliant. But there is a sense conveyed in the coldness of these musical gazes that both felt betrayed by their own musical pasts. They had each become hostile; affronted at the loss of something.

Anyone keen to find out about Cornelius Cardew will quickly discover several things: Firstly, he was regarded as one of the most important composers of his generation, and remains so. In the late-1950s, Karlheinz Stockhausen, a character neither given to self-doubt nor to the over-appreciation of the capabilities of others, employed Cardew as his assistant. Cardew planned and scored substantial sections of Stockhausen's compositions, unsupervised. There is both recognition and exploitation in this.

Secondly, during the early 1970s Cardew fell out publicly and irremediably with his one-time hero, John Cage. Cardew had come to think that both Cage and his works were but flatulent shadows of their former selves. Cardew deplored what he saw as Cage's failure to shuffle over to the interests of the people. He deplored the failure of Cage's later compositions to do more than simply describe the restless surface dynamism of modern society. He deplored their further failure to analyse the causes of such endless, paroxysmal motion. Their once salutary value having faded for him, Cardew thought Cage and his works interesting only instruction-ally, as vehicles of rebuke.

In particular, Cardew thought Cage's anarchism to be not liberatory, but soppy and bourgeois, even deceitful. His complaint was a milieu founding gesture. It was one through which significant figures in British experimental music would come to orient their relationships towards one and other. For his part, and for the rest of his life, Cage remained irritated with Cardew. Cage claimed that Cardew had once refused to properly perform work for which he had employed him. Cage thought Cardew musically unprofessional. Perhaps Cardew cared.

Someone looking would soon find that at some time shortly after 1968, Cardew became an important political activist. He was a founding member of the Revolutionary Communist Party in Britain, and a vigorous promoter of Maoism during the 1970s. He was also friendly with Hardial Bains; who was the founder of the Communist Party of Canada (Marxist/Leninist) and a significant figure in the establishment of Marxist/Leninist organisations, internationally. Cardew set Bains's polemics to music.

Cardew also died in unfortunate, even mysterious circumstances. In 1981, in bad light and bad weather, he was killed in a hit and run incident. Whether this was an accident, a murder or some profound form of suicide has been a subject of speculation ever since. A person might also discover that towards the end of his life Cardew rejected Maoism. This information is detailed in the sleeve notes to a recording of a memorial concert given at the Royal Festival Hall, shortly after his death. It is possibly misleading. What Cardew did, it appears, and this is technical, was to take the Albanian turn. He began supporting the brand of uncompromising Maoism advocated by Enver Hoxha in the period after Mao's death. Correspondingly, with China's splits with first the Soviets, and then Albania, Cardew's thinking continued along Hoxha's interpretation of Maoist lines. Cardew's later disputes with Maoist cultural and political theory – especially over the meaning of Nixon's visit to China in 1972 – have been read conveniently; as a declining of political activism as the force that animated his musical production. Yet, despite the somehow concrete status of these instituted facts, it may be that none of them indicate the nature of Cardew's practice of communism, musically.

~

Snow White invited herself to stay. She left a stew, bubbling and hissing in the fireplace: a rather ungracious kind of rent. They didn't know it yet, but this stew was itself an invitation to the dwarves. It was an invitation to eat, certainly, but this communal meal was also to be a moment of instruction in acceptable decorums of sociability. Perhaps Grumpy showed some prescience. As the pot spat at the dwarves, he warned: 'It's a witch's brew, I tell you.' The dwarves were already in a state of some trepidity. Their anxiousness had been sparked by an unexpected view of their cottage on their return from the mine. They broke from their singing. The windows were lit. This was an alien prospect, and quivering, from behind a fir, they pushed first one then another of their number towards their own front door.

As a concentrated metaphor of radical urban regenera-tion, Snow White represents a recognised kind of action; the flushing out of a population and allowing them back, if at all, only on new and specific terms. Even the birds and bees that burst through the dwarves' window, as an irrepressible and cleansing force of nature, are at Snow White's disposal in this process. The dwarves' quaking return to their newly clean cottage is touching in many ways. The first thing they realise is that perhaps they no longer belong there. At least their old selves don't. Sleepy is in heartbroken dismay at finding the carefully tended accretion of sugar in his tea mug gone. When it is clean, Bashful doesn't even recognise the dwarves' own crockery as crockery. And there is more: the iration of the spiders at having their webs swept away by the Stakhanovite enthusiasm of chipmunks, or that of mice when their homes are filled as improvised rubbish dumps. Each of these discrete sensitivities are ridden over by Snow White's disinterested, commandingly roughshod, musical organisation of labour: *Whistle While You Work*. The pre-existing communal order of the dwarves, robust and grubby in manner, anarcho-syndicalist in principle, never recovered from this state–sanctioned brand of folksy work song.

Rest was Snow White's great danger. It was a noble kiss, of course, which was to eventually save her from endless rest in a glass vitrine. But it was only a human softheartedness that stayed the hand of her would-be murderer, as she lay to appreciate the flowers in a meadow. And mistaken for a ghost or monster, she came within an instant of being bludgeoned to death by the dwarves as she stirred from rest. That reprising moment of her near death at the hands of skilled labour is a terrifying one, but not only for its dramaturgical affects. Disney's attachment of human vitality to a life of specialised, commodifiable toil is part of a greater prescription. This mortally overburdened responsibility of work figures centrally in a preferred model for the bulliable organisation of labour. There is in the narrative of *Snow White* a clearly articulated sense that the sociable worth of individuals may be construed only in terms of their continuing, useful productiveness – and by nothing outside of this. There should be nothing outside of this.

In her role as a monarchical figure of the modern and renewed State, Snow White's own restless busyness is even able to account for the accumulation of the eccentric detritus of a life of labour. Breaking off from labour, preparing not for rest or leisure, but for sleep (in Disney's tale, the only warrantable other of labour), itself requires further labour in the ritualised chores demanded by the maintenance of cleanliness. That aesthetic of excessive cleanliness is both the function and the modern cipher of Snow White's pathologically neurotic relationship to work. After all, it's not as if the dwarves didn't already know to tidy up, and lock away their tools after work.

The stimulation and control of this excess has been remarked upon. In a recent essay on modernist architectural aesthetics, Massimo Cacciari has indicated a small tradition of thought, which has emerged around the meaning of the clean house and the clean window. His suggestion is that a particular critical tradition, one that includes observations on community made by Walter Benjamin and Giorgio Agamben, has noted the capacity of the modernist window to render idiosyncratic, even baffling, the desire to mark and to leave traces of the occupation of modern space. Cacciari's argument is that the maintenance of the aesthetic of the glass wall is predicated on the annihilation of any liking for the informal signs of breaking off from labour, the signs of rest. As an institution (now almost antique, it must be said), modernist cleanliness signals the continuation of work right up to the point of sleep. It also indicates that there is little of value that may emerge, aesthetically or otherwise, from the evidence of the superfluous sociabilities entailed by work. Now, such sociability is recognised as an exploitable resource: the amiable rubbing of shoulders is the principle mechanism of augmented productivity. In the mid 1930s and in the early 1970s, high points of architectural modernism and its images of regulated communality, this was not yet thought so.

We Sing for the Future
'Paragraph 1' of Cardew's *The Great Learning* is divided into sections, each of which is related aesthetically by the fractioning of an excess. There is the choral recitation of Confucius's text, the effectiveness of which, as we have heard, depends in part

on an expected degree of lack in the coordination of speaking voices. The ways that words and fragments of words are produced, their orphaned starts and endings, their delinquent sibilances, the refractory rhythms of murmuring: all of these things are the evidence of a musical sociability. They are materially occupiable as such. The almost unseizable, unrepeatable yet undeniable cadences (which may only be appreciated in the beholdance of a collaborating listener) are of most interest as a political place.

Then there is the whistles chorus: a drone of recorders, ocarinas, swannee whistles, referees' whistles, police whistles, any of the kinds of whistle – all interspersed with virtuoso improvisations on one type of whistle or another. There are similar excesses here, too. But first of all, there is the stones chorus.

For the scoring of the stones chorus Cardew used an invented graphic device which he derived from the forms of Confucius's original chinese characters. It is not quite common notation, but formally similar to it. Cardew was explicit about what should be done. The performers should strike stones together. In doing so, they should take a lead from the rhythmically uneven gestures of a conductor elect. The performers' interpretation of the length of the long tails of each of the notes in the score should guide the loudness of each strike as well as the amplitude of the performer's gestures. These amplitudes determine the moment of arrival of each strike, and as with the recited passage, a pleasing dis-coordination is achieved. The precise textures of the stones chorus are never the same one performance to another. Its affective success is partly secured by the knowledge that each tap is arrived at through some implied democratic negotiation. The scoring, the performance and the sound of the chorus as a whole, is then a philosophical image of communal action.

The scoring of the stones chorus is frank enough, but the epimythic structures of this section of 'Paragraph 1' of *The Great Learning* are equally compelling. Revered percussionist Eddie Prevost, a collaborator with Cardew, has described the legends surrounding the stones chorus. Cardew had found a source of stones with special musical qualities in a quarry in North Yorkshire. Prevost has recalled rain–sodden journeys to the site, driving a vanload of enthusiasts across a wintry and wind–torn landscape to collect the stones. Redolent of a folksy fascination with the mythologies of artisanry, this romance has any number of implications. There is an allegory of resistance to the transparent abilities of industrially produced instruments to contain music, and there is an elegy to the sociabilities of collected labour. There is even a detectable hint at some kind of near-Wagnerian questing – something of the sort that composer Rutland Boughton had earlier reworked in his efforts to establish an English, socialist parallel to the Bayreuth summer festival.

More importantly however, 'Paragraph 1' of *The Great Learning* also served as the reason for the formation of the Scratch Orchestra. This collective of largely untrained musicians, which was convened initially to investigate how to perform *The Great Learning*, represented a model community of social and aesthetic research – an amenity in the production of kinds of uncommodifiable musical and social knowledge. Each member of the orchestra was required to document scratch works in a journal. These works were considered (masterless) apprentice pieces, recounting a process of investigation and experiment. Cardew published many of these apprentice works. As preliminary footnotes to *The Great Learning*, they are revealing of a special relationship to sociability and purposelessness. One such piece, 'Tune a brook by moving the stones in it', is frequently quoted as an example – recognisable perhaps for the way that it resonates with Fluxus sentiments. There are others, each of which signal an indeterminate ambition: 'If inside play the sounds from outside. If outside play the sounds from inside'; 'Moan quietly and sadly, mouth open' or 'Play specific sounds when people leave, enter, speak, look at you'. But perhaps the most indicative of the social-intellectual mien of scratch was this:

> 'Take a mat and a cushion. Arrange instruments within easy reach for playing when lying down. Play, now and then, lying down. Go for a walk to see what others are doing, now and then. Maybe play an instrument while walking'.

On one hand these instructions herald a sense of passivity; one that is evocative of a lazy, summery, English idleness. On the other hand there is a claim made: specifically to rest as the preserve of politically creative endeavour. And it is here where the Scratch Orchestra, as a musically skilled if not musically trained cadre, made its crucial aesthetic discrimination. There is no apostrophe in the stones chorus. Stones are not expected to provide any account of themselves. In the refusal of that small but critical mark lies the acceptance of the entirety of Marx's theorisation of the mysticism of the commodity. Work produces commodities and self-alienation. Association, the product of rest, at least as imagined by scratch sociability, is entirely uncommodifiable.

In his early writings on the theme, Marx described the product of work as a cultural force. He held this product to be a nocive thing, and formative of institutions that are, eventually, both alien and opposed to the subjects of work. Work, then, provides the institutional means via which the value of its subjects may be clearly read, rendered transparent and contained. Snow White is exactly such an institution: she collects work.

~

'And you must be Sleepy'. By collecting work, Snow White collects the dwarves. In co-ordinating the cleaning of the house, she completes her research. When the dwarves eventually muster to present themselves to her, she already knows their names. These little artisans, with their curiously infantilised, bachelor ways, and their adjectival names find themselves subject to a modern anthropology. In the face of the imperial authority of her requirement that they be well-integrated and accepting subjects, the dwarves feel compelled towards hospitability. There was stew to be had, after all. And they sing.

Being Disney of the classic period, in this performance everyone appears to be on board and behaving. But not all are entirely biddable. Bashful, for whatever his deep-seated reasons, finds it difficult to speak or sing. Grumpy refuses to speak civilly. He does not sing. And the libidinally irregulatable Dopey refuses to even try to speak, let alone sing. These intransigences are paralleled by the very incommunicativeness of the *Silly Song* itself – the enigmatic dumbness of the tune, the meaningless of the words. Beaming benevolently, incomprehendingly, with her tinkling laughter Snow White indicates both a patronising accommodation of a cute silliness and a suspicion of the precise and smiling malice that may lay behind it. Snow White's curatorial gaze renders the dwarves' culture anachronistic and unmodern; collectable, yet otherwise purposeless. It might be too that the glance Grumpy shoots at her represents a refusal of her variety of ethnomusicology. He shoots the same glance at his peers and the calliope: which together represent the tradition that allows him to speak at all in this circumstance. Now the *Silly Song* belongs to Snow White. In order to avoid being completely betrayed by their cultural traditions, with a silent and musically extraneous gaze, Grumpy, Bashful and Dopey manage to turn it into a war dance.

In 1972, Cardew denounced publicly the entirety of his own previous musical output. In dealing with *The Great Learning*, he said that Confucius was a reactionary thinker trying to prop up a decadent and dying social system. Of his former self, Cardew said that the composer who in 1968 had decided to follow Pound and the great store that Pound set by his own intelligence, was politically backward and wrapped up in the abstractions of the avant-garde. Of Pound, Cardew noted a reprehensible totalitarianism. Of Pound's translation of Confucius, he pointed to flaws and intellectual deceits. He argued that Pound's concept of 'watching with affection' was a disgraceful advocation of the avoidance of political responsibility. The idea of observing in repose 'the struggles of the people', as if through a window was an anathema to him.

Earlier that year, the BBC had offered the opportunity for the Scratch Orchestra to perform 'Paragraph 1' of *The Great Learning* as one of the Promenade Concerts. Cardew suggested a retranslation of the spoken passage:

> '*The Great Learning* means raising your level of consciousness by getting right to the heart of a matter and acting on your conclusions. *The Great Learning* is rooted in love for the broad masses of the people. The target of *The Great Learning* is justice and equality, the highest good for all.'

Cardew complained of the BBC's removal of banners bearing slogans from the concert stage. He spoke too of a better 'disciplined' rendition of the work. But what is important in this is that the aleatory effects of choral cadence in the speaking of these revised words remained. Despite the changes in the outward appearance of aspects of Cardew's stated political and aesthetic principles, Cardew never deserted this device. A question that he had put in 1968 – 'What is there in uselessness to cause you distress?' – remained as a sociable and musical means to produce unmarketable, unrepeatable, uncommodifiable excess. It is through this formulation of excess, one opposed to Snow White's, that Cardew maintained a particular ethic of improvisation. It was an ethic whose plebiscitary appeal was made in bypassing the containing boundaries of accepted or even merely recognisable musical forms.

When Bashful, Dopey and Grumpy were invited to improvise about a theme – vocally, percussively and at the calliope, respectively – their brilliances were musically constrained by a form which they saw pass in that instant from their ownership to Snow White's. Their glances, illegible by definition, are all that remained to surpass that form. In clear senses, the translation and conservation of that glance as a musical possibility is the centre of Cardew's practice of communism.

Even when Cardew set Hardial Bain's self-consciously ugly polemic poetry to music, he succeeded in this. The best loved of his Bains settings, *We Sing for the Future*, exercises a specific impossibility. The chorus runs so:

> 'We sing for the future
> Proletarians of all lands
> We unite and fight together
> For the victory of communism'

That victory of a musical communism lies in a refusal to be interpreted. No matter how technically accomplished, no singer and no chorus can pull all these words into the framework of the tune Cardew supplied for them. These words burst the musical vitrine that tries to contain them. The excess, ever-changing, is a site and a fleeting deposit of a type of communist sociability; something to be cherished and inhabited. Moreover, that image of the failure of a collectable folk tune to contain and to harmonise the sentiments and textures of Bains's words also represents a challenge. It is a challenge to anthropological understandings of work.

Coda: Useless Work Songs

Hi-Ho! A note called – hi – followed by another, one octave above – ho. In this, the dwarves' call to labour, a specific and mystical relationship is articulated. The octaval interval has a metonymic association with the all-encompassing appeal made by a powerful musical image of social cohesiveness, the diapason. The diapason is the imagined sound of everything in natural and divine harmony. But the ability of the diapason to mystically conjure a relation between everything as a form of omniscience, is itself neurotic. It rests on the illusion, or rather the conceit that all things may connect, and be apprehended in the mysteriousness of their connection. It is a political image of a particular representative order, not unlike the plenum or plebiscite. In some senses, it is the very expectation articulated by the dwarves' call to labour that they will be understood, that reduces Grumpy to wordlessness in his moment of great cultural calamity. It is in this musical relationship that the entirety of Disney's prescription of a happy, bulliable, anarcho-syndicalist organisation of creative labour truly resides – in a mine where a million diamonds shine.

Against a background of bells and picks and hammers, Disney's composer-librettists Frank Churchill and Larry Morey never allow the dwarves to sing the octave chordally. They are not given anything that may indicate the excesses of what may be called truly choral. There is only a call and a response; an interpellation, a hailing. The sentimental individuality of each toiling voice is preserved in the choir, isolatable and oppressable. In fact, the more truly representative acoustic register here is the transparent chime heard when, with a well-schooled blow, bespeaking a specialised somatic education, a recently mined gem is struck to test for its unique perfections.

It is perhaps this implication of a meek failure in anarchist politics and economics, as well as its predisposition towards totalitarianism in times of calamity, which lay behind Cardew's dismissal of John Cage's musical anarchism. For on some points they remained in agreement – even if they could not say so to each other. One of the many anecdotes that John Cage recounted in his autobiographically structured work *Indeterminacy*, refers to a special skill. A mutual friend had sent to both him, and the pianist David Tudor, packages of spice, beans and palm sugar. The parcels had become damaged in transit, and the contents hopelessly mixed. Tudor went through his own parcel, scrupulously separating each speck of spice and sugar from the beans. Tudor offered to similarly sort through Cage's package. In telling of this, Cage had clearly seen the way that Tudor had identified and quietly refined some brilliant technical facility. Cage declined Tudor's offer to repair his gift, though. And in doing this he signified a desire to preserve such an unwarranted skill from the deleterious effects of an economy, no matter how tiny, esoteric or personal that economy may remain. About this kind of unprofessional, unrepeatable irregularity, Cardew cared enormously.

TO THE STUDENTS OF KENT STATE
Sarah Pierce/The Metropolitan Complex

1.

2.

3.

4.

7.

ASSOCIATED STUDENTS
OF THE
UNIVERSITY OF COLORADO
BOULDER. COLORADO 80302

Dear Sir,

The following resolution was consigned by every member of the Student Senate of the University of Colorado that was present at the May 5, 1970 meeting.

Whereas the Ohio National Guard is trained in riot-control, fully armed and protected with battlefield uniform, gasmasks, and bayonets, and,

Whereas the National Guard has been called out in California and Chicago in the event of student riots, and no deaths have been caused by National Guardsmen firing on students, and

Whereas the Ohio State Highway Patrol denies having seen a sniper on a campus building, and

Whereas students deny the charge made by the National Guard that there was a sniper; and no students were armed except one newspaper reporter, and

Whereas the National Guard claimed self-defense in the act of firing into an unarmed, disorganized crowd of students protesting the Indo-Chinese War, and

Whereas the Ohio National Guard, after running out of tear gas, and "returning fire" in defense of their lives remained in military formation and shot to death the following Kent State students: Miss Allison Krause, 19; Miss Sandy Lee Scheuer, 20; Jeffery G. Miller, 20; and William K. Schroeder, 19; with possibly more dead; and wounding twelve; while no National Guardsmen were wounded or injured despite their claim of self-defense.

Therefore Be It Resolved,
1) That the A.S.U.C. Senate condemn the actions of the Governor of Ohio, James A. Rhodes; the administration of Kent University; and the Ohio National Guard, and

2) That the four students of Kent State will have not have died in vain.

Peace,

John W. Everitt

John W. Everitt
President of ASUC

8.

To the students of Kent State
1-7. Audiences, Student Cultural Centre (SKC)
April Meeting Belgrade, former Yugoslavia,
c. 1972

8. Letter to the students of Kent State
University from the Colorado Associated
Students, Boulder, Colorado, 5 May 1970

9. Students gathered at Victory Bell, Kent
State University, Kent, Ohio, 1 May 1970

Special thanks to the May 4 Collection, Kent
State University Libraries and Media
Services, Department of Special Collections
and Archives; and the Studentski Kulturi
Centar (SKC) Archive, Belgrade

9.

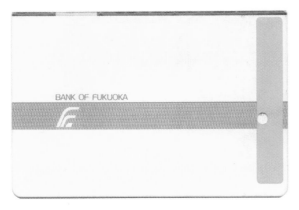

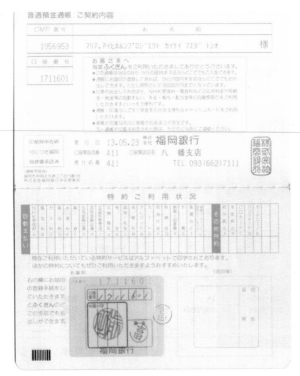

• *Bank book, outside and inside cover*
Japanese banks use bank books which show details of all transactions. On the outside cover of the bank book are the branch number of the bank (411), the account number (1711601), the title 'Maria Eichhorn Project' and the name of the account holder, Maeda Toshio. The inside cover of the bank book also gives the date the account was opened, 23 May 2001 (13.05.23 according to the Japanese calendar), as well as further details about the account.

JOINT ACCOUNT NO. 1711601, BANK OF FUKUOKA, YAHATA BRANCH 411
Maria Eichhorn

The Yokohama 2001: International Triennale of Contemporary Art took place from 2 September to 11 November 2001 under the main theme 'Mega Wave – Towards a New Synthesis'. The port city of Yokohama is the second largest city in Japan, within commuting distance of Tokyo. Works by over a hundred artists were shown in a variety of locations; in addition symposiums, workshops and other events were held. The exhibition was mainly housed in the Pacifico Yokohama Exhibition Hall, part of the recently built National Convention Hall, and the historic Red Brick Warehouse. They are located directly on the harbour front in the gentrified district of Minato Mirai Shinko. The exhibition was financed by the Japan Foundation, the city of Yokohama, Japan Public Broadcasting Corporation and the Asahi Shimbun newspaper.

2001 saw an economic, social and political change of direction in Japan. Junichiro Koizumi (from the LDP – Liberal Democratic Party) was elected as the new prime minister, on a platform of ending state subsidy programmes, accelerated reforms of the financial markets and privatisation of the postal savings system. The latter had been used by the ruling LDP up to that point as a way of financing measures to stimulate the economy. Those still against privatisation include to this day the social democrats, the communists and some defectors from the LDP. The unemployment rate reached 5% in July 2001, the highest level since 1945. There were also increasing levels of homelessness. Koizumi visited the Yusukuni Shrine, which honours war dead, on 21 August 2001. Parliament passed a law on 18 October that year, allowing Japanese soldiers to serve abroad for the first time since the Second World War.

Nobuo Nakamura and Akiko Miyake head the Center for Contemporary Art (CCA) in Kitakyushu, which they founded and opened in May 1997. With financial backing from the city, the programme includes a postgraduate degree programme, a comprehensive library, an exhibition hall and a series of art book publications. I taught at the CCA as a guest professor in June 1998, continuing my project *Curtain (Denim) / Lectures by Yuko Fujita, Mika Obayashi*. Following the exhibition *Maria Eichhorn, Curtain (Denim) / Lectures by Yuko Fujita, Mika Obayashi* (1989/1997–98) was published.

The first Yokohama Triennale took place in 2001. Four curators organised four distinct and independent sections. I took part in the section curated by Nobuo Nakamura. With Akiko Miyake as project manager, he invited a number of international artists to participate. Both Nakamura and Miyake had worked with many of these previously at the Center for Contemporary Art in Kitakyushu. The Triennale was aimed specifically at new works of art.

My idea for the Yokohama Triennale was to use my production budget to open a joint bank account, which would be freely available to all. An account was opened at the Bank of Fukuoka in May 2001, several months before the exhibition was due to begin. At the same time the Maeda Accounting Office, based in Kitakyushu, was authorised to deal with administering the account and any ensuing correspondence.

The only object in the 30m^2 booth at the exhibition was a plexiglas container along the back wall with a leaflet which visitors were invited to take with them. The leaflet contained the following explanation and the conditions (in Japanese and English) for participating in the joint account.

Maria Eichhorn Joint Account No. 1711601, Bank of Fukuoka, Yahata Branch 411 (2001)

On 23 May 2001 an open-access account was set up in Yahata: Account No. 1711601, Bank of Fukuoka, Yahata Branch 411

The setting-up of this account is based on the idea of people acting for the common good, with each participant being equally responsible for their own transactions and for the account as a whole. This applies as much to individual payments and transfers into the account as it does to individual withdrawals from the account.

Transfers from other accounts or cash payments into the above-named account may be carried out by any participant. Transfers from the above-named to other accounts are made by a specially authorised person. For money to be transferred from the account, an application marked 'Joint Account' stating the amount required, the name, address and bank details of the recipient should be sent to:

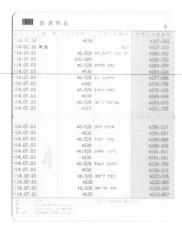

• *Bank book, page 2*
The dates when money was transferred (using the Japanese calendar) are given in the column on the left. Withdrawals are listed in the third column and deposits in the fourth. The names of the depositor or payee are to the left or right of the amount. The account balance is in the right hand column. The highest amount withdrawn from the joint account was ¥ 300,000. This amount was transferred back into the joint account by the same person twelve days later.

• *Bank book, page 3*
The top half lists mainly deposits; the bottom half lists only withdrawals complete with the transfer fee of ¥ 630. At the top, four participants transferred ¥ 500, ¥ 2,000, ¥ 333 and ¥ 2,964 to the joint account. At the bottom, the same four people transferred ¥ 333, ¥ 1,500, ¥ 500 and ¥ 2,967 back from the joint account to their own accounts.

• *Bank book, page 4*
Twenty-one participants received ¥ 6,528 each after the project ended. Transferring the money to Finland cost ¥ 10,000 in fees, compared with the ¥ 630 fee for most of the domestic transfers.

• *Bank book, page 5*
The last transfer to a participant's bank account in the USA (transfer fee ¥ 10,000). Transfer of the remaining balance, ¥ 137,090, to an account belonging to the Taiyo Pan bakery in Kitakyushu. The joint account was closed on 4 July 2002 (14.07.04 acording to the Japanese calendar).

• *Bank book, page 6*
No entries

Maeda Toshio, 2-6-8 Iwaimachi, Yahata-higashi-ku,
Kitakyushu 805-0041

The start-up capital in the above-named account is
¥ 800,000. This sum is part of the production budget
available to Maria Eichhorn for her contribution to the
Yokohama Triennial.

The account is open from 2 September until 11 November
2001. On its dissolution, should there be sufficient funds,
the monies held in that account will be divided and equal
amounts transferred into the accounts of all the partici-
pants.

The participants agree to the following conditions: ap-
plications will be processed in order of their arrival. Only
applications containing all the required information will
be considered. Transfers from the above-named account
to other accounts are only possible if sufficient funds are
available. All transfer activities will be registered for the
purposes of Maria Eichhorn's work Joint Account No.
1711601, Bank of Fukuoka, Yahata Branch 411 *and may*
be published.

As noted in the leaflet the initial deposit was ¥ 800,000
(then worth about US $ 6,700). This was the amount
remaining from the production budget once the printing
costs for the 20,000 leaflets had been deducted.

Before the project began,
it was arranged that Toshio Maeda from the Maeda Accounting Office would respond to all applications for
money transfers individually and personally. Each letter
of reply would include a copy of the current bank statement. The idea was that just sending an application to
the Accounting Office would be sufficient to make somebody a joint account holder, and the applicant would
consequently receive the details of the bank balance.

Three possible cases were
identified in relation to the processing of transfers and
replying to applications:

Case A – the amount requested is available and trans-
ferred
Case B – the account has no available funds
Case C – the amount requested is higher than the avail-
able funds

Appropriate sample let-
ters were prepared for these three cases. For case A (the
amount requested is available and transferred):

'Dear . . . (participant's name) . . .,

Thank you for your application.
The amount of . . . (amount) . . . which you requested was
transferred on . . . (date) . . . to your account number . . .
(account number) . . .'Please see the enclosed bank state-
ment for details.

Thank you for participating in Maria Eichhorn's work
Joint Account No. 1711601, Bank of Fukuoka, Yahata
Branch 411 *(2001).*

Best wishes,
Maeda Toshio'

Sample letters were also
written for cases B and C, with the addition of the relevant information on the account balance. For situation
B (the account has no available funds):

'[. . .] The account has no available funds at the moment.
Please see the enclosed bank statement for details. We
would like to request that you try again later [. . .].'

For case C (the amount
requested is higher than the available funds):

'[. . .] The amount you have requested is currently not
available. Please see the enclosed bank statement for
details. [. . .]'

An analysis of transac-
tions to and from the joint account as well as applications
made to the Accounting Office shows that more transfers
were made to the joint account than from the joint account to the participants' accounts; however the transfers
to the joint account had a total value which was lower
than those from the account. Thirty-one people transferred money to the joint account thirty-seven times; two
of these people made multiple transfers – one person
six times and the second twice. The six transfers were of
¥ 11, 22, 9, 4, 2 and concluded once more with ¥ 11. The
second participant transferred ¥ 3,000 and ¥ 1,000.

Money was transferred
from the joint account to other accounts sixteen times.
Three participants received money on two occasions,
with one of them receiving a total of ¥ 250,000, ¥ 100,000
and ¥ 150,000 respectively. The amount of ¥ 150,000 was
the second highest to be requested and transferred. The
second of these three participants obtained firstly ¥ 4,444

and then ¥ 40,000. The third participant made three applications of varying amounts to the Accounting Office; ¥ 30,000 and ¥ 147,309 were transferred to his account. His third application for ¥ 17,035 could not be complied with as the joint account did not have sufficient funds at the time the application was made. For this same reason it was not possible to process three further applications from other participants.

The period where the account did not have sufficient funds came at the beginning of the project, when almost without exception relatively high sums of money were transferred from the joint account to the participants' accounts (between 26 September and 12 October 2001), but before the highest amount taken from the joint account – ¥ 300,000 – was transferred back (it was debited from the joint account on 12 October and returned on 24 October 2001).

Five transactions took place in the other direction. The following amounts were initially transferred to the joint account and later back to their original accounts: ¥ 3,000 credited and ¥ 2,685 debited; ¥ 500 credited and ¥ 500 debited; ¥ 2,000 credited and ¥ 1,500 debited; ¥ 333 credited and ¥ 333 debited; ¥ 2,964 credited and ¥ 2,967 debited. One participant requested ¥ 1,000, having previously deposited ¥ 3,000 in the joint account. It was not possible to comply with this as the account did not at that time have sufficient funds.

Six of the thirty-one participants who deposited money in the joint account later wanted money back (in one case this was not complied with). Including the participant who later transferred the ¥ 300,000 he had received back to the joint account, six participants were both payer and payee; in three cases (¥ 300,000, ¥ 333 and ¥ 500) the amounts transferred were identical.

Although many transactions used deliberately conspicuous combinations of numbers (4,444, 33,333, 333, 111), the majority of transfers were of round numbers (five times ¥ 500, eleven times ¥ 1,000, twice ¥ 2,000, three times ¥ 3,000 and once ¥ 10,000). The highest amount recorded was ¥ 300,000 and the second highest was ¥ 20,980.

During the course of the project (which lasted as long as the exhibition), there were thirty-seven deposits to the joint account and sixteen withdrawals. The combined deposits added up to less than the withdrawals; consequently ¥ 307,283 remained at the end of the exhibition from the original sum of ¥ 800,000.

A letter was to be sent to each participant at the end of the project. Two alternative situations were anticipated:

Case 1 – if there are sufficient funds the amount will be divided into equal parts and transferred to all participants.

Case 2 – the account has no available funds

Sample letters for both cases were drafted at the start of the project.

A total of forty-two people took part in the project. Thirty-seven people were directly involved in account transactions, six of whom both deposited and withdrew money. Five participants either made applications when there were insufficient funds, made applications without requests for money to the Accounting Office, or applied after the end of the exhibition.

The account numbers and addresses of those people who made applications to the Accounting Office were known, but not the bank details of those who had paid into the joint account without making withdrawals. The account holders' banks did not reveal the account numbers of those making deposits. It was only possible to see the depositors' names, which were listed in the bank book next to the amount deposited. For this reason the account numbers and addresses of twenty-one depositors – from a total of thirty-one – remained unknown.

The account details of twenty-one people were known, eighteen of whom had sent applications to the Accounting Office. In three cases people whose names were known had transferred money to the joint account without first making an application. To sum up, twenty-one names came complete with account details and addresses, twenty-one names were without.

When the project ended twenty-one participants received a letter containing a concluding report and final account statement. The final balance of ¥ 307,283 was divided by forty-two and twenty-one participants received ¥ 6,528 each. Once the bank fees had been deducted, the remaining ¥ 137,090 was donated to the Taiyo Pan bakery in Kitakyushu. The joint account was closed on 4 July 2002.

The participants received more information on the Taiyo Pan bakery in the final letter of the project of 7 July 2002: 'This bakery was established fifteen years ago; on its staff were four young people with special needs. Today sixteen people with Down's syndrome work at the bakery, on a profit-sharing basis, producing bread and biscuits free of (chemical) additives.'

Without the assistance of Akiko Miyake, who persuaded Toshio Maeda to manage the bookkeeping and correspondence with the participants for no fee, this project would not have been possible. I am enormously grateful to both of them. My thanks go to all the participants in the project, as well as Nobuo Nakamura for inviting me to the Yokohama Triennale. Finally I would like to thank Gavin Everall, Gerrie van Noord, Grant Watson, Marius Babias.

THE BIG GIFTING
Klaus Weber

CONSIDERING THE SOCIAL,
A CONVERSATION ON COMMUNITY
Martha Rosler with Ayreen Anastas and
Rene Gabri of 16Beaver

Ayreen Anastas/Rene Gabri: *Dear Martha, We thought it would be nice to begin this interview by citing another inquiry on Communism initiated by Jean-Luc Nancy in the 1980s in his book* The Inoperative Community. *In that book, he attempts, amongst other things, to acknowledge and engage with the failures of communism. More importantly, although it was written before the fall of the Berlin Wall, he sees the reduction of politics to purely economic and technical forces, to order and administration within an assumed consensus. He argues that speaking from the left would at the very least mean 'that the political, as such, is receptive to what is at stake in community.' And he goes on to state that the 'political is indissociable from something that the word "communism" has expressed too poorly, even as it remains the only word to point toward it...' It seems that today as we witness the global spread of neo-liberal ideology alongside a neo-imperialist resurgence in the US, such a distinction is helpful, because it opens the space for seeing what may be at stake in politics.*

Martha Rosler: Nancy appears to be articulating what many on the left – especially the self-described democratic left – have also remarked on: that what is at stake in politics and the shared struggle was not enhanced by the articulation of collectivism of the Soviet state and its satellite parties elsewhere. To take up Nancy's point about the reduction of politics to order and administration: In the most sharply defined instances, order (policing and military force) and administration (bureaucracy) are the defining functions of a state in which the legal system is concerned not with rights but with enforcement; the state in effect defends itself from below, from its own people, in other words, for whom power is supposedly exercised. This form of sovereignty is reminiscent of the monarchic 'representation' referred to by Habermas in his famous encyclopaedia article on the public sphere, where, before the development of this sphere, the voice of the people is presumed to be embodied in the ruler and there is in fact no mechanism for *vox populi* actually to be heard.[1] In effect, if not in intent, this curbs the notion of the individual citizen as a valid position from which to petition the government on either private or public matters. The individual has no valid voice nor any opportunity to articulate a voice within any recognised 'community' or public sphere: A state preoccupied with administration similarly cannot but regard the individual as what we might call a 'de-subjectivised subject', an entity whose primary recognition by the state is as a being subject to, falling under, its rules – rules, of course, from which it itself is largely exempt.[2]

In *On Violence* (1969), Hannah Arendt writes: 'The transformation of government into administration, or of republics into bureaucracies, and the disastrous shrinkage of the public realm that went with it have a long and complicated history throughout the modern age; and this process has been considerably accelerated during the last hundred years through the rise of party bureaucracies.'[3]

In states that do not recognise or respect individual rights – but not only there – grass-roots politics turns to a collective, anti-state movement, while the sanctioned political process carries on with business as usual.

Governments formed as the result of revolutions or revolutionary movements assume that they are at the pinnacle of a community that demands control of all elements of the state and society and their complete reform or replacement. In practice this amounts to the suspension of the normal rule of law, producing a state of exception that begins to seem like (or to become) tyranny as it becomes normalised. It is a real question, then, how long such states of exception ought to last, because (if nothing else) they can easily become points of attack for the enemies. Even leaders who are democratically elected, such as Venezuela's Hugo Chávez or Chile's Salvador Allende, and who have not suspended the rule of law but have announced a new agenda for the distribution of social resources, have been attacked as dictators, despite their demonstrable popularity with their electorates. They are attacked from without, by the United States, and from within by those who formerly wielded power – the ruling oligarchic elite – as dictatorial because they have discarded the unspoken rules and transgressed against the consensuses of rulership. They are in effect traitors to their class or the class they were meant to join upon election as head of state and have become 'outsiders' and populists, in which populism is understood in the European sense to mean demagoguery.

Just at the moment in which their opponents are excoriating them for being dangerously 'emotional', it is clear that these leaders are in fact perceived as all too rational, for they stand at the head of radical popular – grass-roots – movements of the poor and disenfranchised demanding their rights. These movements, whatever one might say of them, have their facts and figures well in hand. At the same time, there are elsewhere in the world many grass-roots movements based on social prejudice, on demonstrably false social assertions, on political dogmas, and, of course, on the metaphysical: namely, religion. In the United States, the religious right bears obvious parallels to other radical popular – grass-roots – movements abroad. It has not, however, succeeded in replacing the state, only in taking over important elements. Its most deeply 'fundamentalist' elements nevertheless wish to theologise the state, much like the pan-Islamicists.

In some ways these popular Islamicist movements in the East reflect the situation described by Hannah Arendt in her book *On Totalitarianism*, in the chapters on 'pan movements' that characterised Continental European imperialism from about the turn of the twentieth century to the Second World War. Movements represent themselves as 'above party' and also, if possible, as 'above the state'. Arendt – whom I am re-reading because of her up-coming centennial – remarks that by the outbreak of the Second World War, and consequent on Hitler's rise to power, all European democracies had adopted some form of dictatorship as a response, but ultimately these dictatorships were powerless to stop the force of either the anti-state movements or Hitler. In the democracies, the existing parties had split in relation to the question of whether to go to war against Germany, and these splits, and policy reversals, undermined the 'identities' of these parties, whose existence had been the protection within state government of specific interest groups. In Europe these dictatorships were not military dictatorships, as they often have been elsewhere, and Arendt traces the fall of the European states precisely to the inability of the military to take them over, for that paradoxically left the state as the mediator between parties rather than standing above them. Finally, both state and parties united to preserve the status quo, but that simply left them vulnerable to collapse in the face of extra-party (and extra-state) movements.[4] In the present situation in the Greater Middle East (and beyond), many of the Muslim-majority nations have adopted or have been instituted as dictatorships – and in this case they are indeed military dictatorships, or the military is always at the ready to take over (as it did in Pakistan and, earlier, in Turkey) – or more-or-less absolute monarchies even if with electoral trappings, banning certain popular movements, and the parties they form, from political participation and even going so far (in the case of Algeria) as to nullify elections.

In Algeria in 1991-1992, in the face of an election victory by an Islamic party, the FIS (Islamic Salvation Front), the next round of elections was cancelled and a state of emergency declared by the military. The argument put forward by secularists is that in refusing to allow a theocratic party representing a pan-Islamist position (in distinction to the secular pan-Arabism of previous decades) to win the election, the state was preserving itself as a secular state and thereby defending the rule of democracy in the face of an absolutist movement: Democracy is defended by suspending the rule of law, both internally and externally.[5] The election victory of Hamas (Islamic Resistance Movement) in the Occupied Territories of Palestine in 2006 was deemed unacceptable by Israel and the US, which have labelled Hamas a terrorist organisation.[6] What is often left out of these accounts is the road to ascendancy of Islamist movements, which occurred as the secularist, often Marxist or socialist, movements, including leading elements of pan-Arabism, were repressed and their leaders persecuted, imprisoned, or killed by the ruling governments. These movements were filling a vacuum of organised resistance, but in addition they were often covertly fostered by those same governments as a counterforce – one that now, decades later, has produced a terrifying 'blowback'. The most widely acknowledged example is the Afghan mujahedeen, formed under Osama Bin Laden and others with the muscular support of the CIA, but Hamas was also supported (some say, formed) by the Israeli security forces to counter the Palestinian left, which was actively repressed. It is community need that is supported by these movements, including material need alongside an ideological identity of self-organisation and resistance.

In their book, Afflicted Powers, *Retort actually argue that 'It is only Islam, for now at least – that can claim to provide a political project that is global in reach and ambition, anti-imperialist (in some of its expressions) and revolutionary in practice.' How in fact can the Left (in all its fragments) pick up the pieces and imagine a political community today?[7] One of the suggestions that Nancy makes is that at the core of politics is a struggle for being-in-common and being together which would be juxtaposed to community as 'being common', being of togetherness or the community as a single entity, e.g. body, mind, fatherland.[8]*

A 'community of interest', rather than a simple geographical collection of people, seems to be what people often mean when they invoke community. The movements I have described each posit a community organised above factions and squabbling, above parties and states, and occasionally even above race, with characteristics rather like the 'imagined community' that Benedict Anderson described as lying at the heart of modern nationalism.[9] Present notions of community seem to be sub-cultural (identitarian, recreational, et cetera), religious, or reactionary, or a combination of those, and indeed the relation of identity to community is an important area to attempt to define.[10] Grass-roots political movements, which can be on the left or the right, may define their community over and against political, cultural, or corporate elites. In any case, the term 'communism' is a clear indication that community has been an important element of left-wing politics. A unifying concept of universal rights as a basis of community is in some respects at cross-purposes to Marxist notions of the universality of working-class, or proletarian, interests. Leftism as manifested by young activists, such as those in the anti-(corporate-)globalisation movements, seems to be a form of vaguely delineated anarchic communitarianism, a kind of beloved community, to use a religious term favoured by Martin Luther King. This reminds me very much of the situation in the early 1960s, before the rediscovery by the American 'New Left' not only of its predecessors in the 'Old Left', that of organised groups like the Communist Party and the various Trotskyist parties, but also of Marx's writings and European commentaries on them (not to mention Marcuse and the Frankfurt School and other varieties of *Kulturkritik*, and Francophone theorists starting with Roland Barthes and Anglophones such as Marshall McLuhan and Stuart Hall and the Birmingham School, all of whom reintroduced versions of community that departed from both religion and American structural-functionalist sociology that was centred on small towns). Another horizon for change rests with the so-called micro-movements, often centred on net culture. As Brian Holmes has suggested, these include such disruptive or destabilising movements as Al Qaida, open-source hackers, and also financial operators.[11]

In thinking about this interview, we picked up a few earlier books that include your own writings. One of them was a book entitled Discussions in Contemporary Culture *edited by Hal Foster. The first discussion is between yourself, Craig Owens, and Thomas Crow. We actually read it together in our early reading groups at 16Beaver. Amongst the various points that are raised is this collapse from a notion of a public to one of audience within the art context. Unfortunately, this slip has only seemed to worsen. Many museums and art spaces today (like most television networks) fail to make this distinction between audience and public. Have you anything to add to the thoughts and questions raised in those discussions given that today one could without great effort expand the discussion of that slippage to spheres outside of cultural production – for example, in relation to the city and public space. Today we are increasingly being asked to experience our own cities as 'tourists', as consumers, as a kind of 'audience' or 'spectator' not as a constituent element or public. One could look at specific mediums you have worked with or projects you have initiated as attempts to thwart these trends or to reclaim something from the notion of public – of participation, of disagreement, of contestation, of sharing, of a commons, if audience opens up associations with consumption, with spectacle, with passivity. What has been your working notion of 'public'?*

The spectacularisation of culture is proceeding as predicted, since that discussion of the public sphere in which I participated in the early 1980s. Advanced industrial societies have continued with the integration of industrialised culture, a process that extends to every possible level of culture, from the lowest and least socially regarded to the most elite, and even those distinctions have only limited meaning that I won't dissect here. The culture industry is of special importance not only to the economy of the United States but also to the maintenance of social order, to maintaining consensus about our common perceptions of ourselves; it is at the heart of our identity. Henri Lefebvre, amongst others, has pointed out the way in which modern societies in the West (I think he traced it, following a Weberian theme, to Protestantism) have replaced external social controls with internalised ones, which are far superior in that the individual recognises the ideas in question as part of her/himself and thus freely chosen and related to self-identification. The old-style totalitarianism of harsh laws is far inferior to this. I have suggested elsewhere that in our society the arts, symbolising the 'freedom' of individual subjectivity, cannot avoid complicity with power groups. You refer to the way we have been turned into tourists in our own land, in our own cities. The city is at the heart of the spectacular regime and is both actual and virtual. Former mayor Giuliani – a good 'little fascist' – was in excellent control over this transformation of New York; he knew how to be the right kind of authoritarian to engineer this change, even becoming the Good Father (as opposed to his usual stance as the punisher) during the terrible events of 11 September 2001. Amongst his first public pronouncements was to exhort us New Yorkers to 'Go out and shop'. He made particular mention of theatres (he and the state governor even made television commercials staged in the heart of Times Square, the heart of the theatre district as well as the epicentre of New York's spectacle of light and commerce), in part because in virtually all traditional cultures bereavement seriously restricts entertainment and celebration in favour of mourning rituals. I will leave the further interpretation of that exhortation to another time, but certainly it went far to define our core identities as consumers, and that of spectacles in particular. The population in general is constantly being propagandised about the meanings of our own experience, not to mention of the actions of the state: witness the ever-mutating rationales for the war in Iraq and perhaps beyond, which do not seem to de-legitimise the Bush administration in the eyes of much of the population. It is assumed that the strong leader has a reason for his actions, even if unwilling to share them with the little people (shades of Straussian neo-conservatism!).

As to the spectacularisation of museum culture, a good resource is *Whose Muse?*, a published discussion amongst the heads of several major museums in the US and Britain, in which non-attendees Tom Krens of the Guggenheim franchise and Arnold Lehman of the Brooklyn Museum are the spectres who haunt the discussion, as exponents of extreme moves into (presumably inauthentic and excessively demotic) entertainment culture. I sympathise with the complaints of the museum directors, up to a point.[12]

But I think that there is always an opening for an art of critique. I believe that art, contrary to the position of conservative defenders of eternal verities and universal forms in art, is illegible, finally, outside the context of reception. Art is a form of symbolic communication, and thus it makes no sense to suggest anything different, unless you are a Platonist. It may be what is behind the sleight-of-hand transformation of the transcendent ideals of such art from the Sublime to simply the Beautiful, or more domestically (so to speak) Beauty, which reveals it to be, ultimately, formalist aestheticism, received through a non-cognitive faculty (cf. Kant). Because symbolic behaviour is regularised, it should be easy to impose a disruption, although the strong efforts of most of the elements (internalised ones!) of the systems of reception will work to pull the behaviour into the centre and thus mute its meaning. The question is whether the disruption will be either legible or intelligible. After all, it is easy to misperceive the *modus operandi*, the goals, and even the effects of disrupters. Have a plan in place is the strategy for substantive political change. Consistently enunciating a coherent critique is the necessary accompaniment that artists and others need to take to heart. The tactics may shift, and even the strategy, but one at least knows what is at stake.

Can you speak about a specific project and insights it may offer for this discussion? Has your own notion of a public changed since the 1960s?

To illustrate the need for flexibility, not to say mobility, let me talk about my anti-war montage project, called *Bringing the War Home: House Beautiful*.[13] This series grew out of a much less focused group of montages I was making quite early, in the mid-1960s, which mostly had to do with images of women, including paintings, photos, and most of all advertising. At some point it occurred to me that the photomontage form was eminently adaptable to images about the war in Vietnam. But I refused to consider this as gallery art. At the time, it would have inevitably been seen as ironic Pop Art. The alternative was as simple propaganda, in an uncontrolled 'flow' of images. All right, I decided, if this is propaganda, let's hope it can help mobilise people. But I would distribute them only on the street, in lousy Xerox copies, and finally I published some in the underground press, when I moved to San Diego in the late 1960s. I felt that to exhibit them in an art institution – as I was asked to do – would have been obscene, since it would have transformed the images of victims of an on-going conflict into art. Art at that time had no room for topical, political speech, as I have suggested, and that included both gallery and museum culture. There was, however, a very extensive and powerful 'counterculture', with hundreds of newspapers and other organs around the country – including the Pacifica radio network (whose New York radio station, WBAI, had one hour of on-the-scene reporting from Vietnam every night, *The War Report* with Dale Minor, which told me all I needed to know). My rejection of museum exhibition, by the way, was not intended to be a blanket refusal, and indeed I had shown paintings in a gallery or two and sold a few, and I was making work specifically intended to be shown in museums and galleries, including a photo-text work called *The Bowery in two inadequate descriptive systems*. I was also producing mail works, which were extra-institutional but sent to people in and outside those institutions.

All of these works were, in their way, disruptive of the expectations of their media. When the Bush administration began to move towards war in Iraq, in 2002, my first impulse was to join with other people in street protests and also with other artists trying to figure out how to oppose the war as artists. I also felt, by 2003, a need to return to the montage format – to oppose the war, of course, but I was also offering a meta-comment, that the country was going to follow the Vietnam playbook of invading a country with little apparent ability to resist the fantastic US war machine but would wind up in the same Big Muddy, bogged down in an unwinnable debacle, and thus I should do a new series of antiwar montages, just like the old series.

Then I had to ask myself where to put any new montages, and I made a different choice about the mode of dissemination. The art world has changed quite a bit since the 1960s and 1970s. It has incorporated many culture-industry norms. Visitors to art institutions have greatly increased in number, and there are many more people calling themselves artists. The art world has been drawn deeper into the generalised system of publicity and celebrity formation, but the widened defini-tion of what art institutions will accept – sometimes including what had formerly been rigorously excluded as topical and agitational – means that museum-goers could expect to see overtly critical work (after all, even television drama has become openly topical if not admittedly partisan in respect to the war). Taking all this into consideration, I decid-ed, this time around, to place my new montages in gallery and museum venues, where they would join exemplars of the earlier Vietnam series.[14] The de-politicisation of the early series, I believed, would be interrupted and, at the same time, the first series would lend legitimacy and resonance to the new group. Since I am now much more 'visible' in-ternationally, I also felt that showing the works inside the art world would probably lead to their immediate reproduction in mass media. I was correct about this, especially in Europe, and especially in the German-speaking countries. Contemplating the change in tactics presented me with an uncertain situation, but that was what I ultimately decided to do. The works are also available on the Internet, and one has been made into a poster.

To explain a bit more about how I think the art world has changed its view of what gets through the gates, let me begin by saying that Pop changed the art world and conceptualism changed it further. Both benefited from systems analysis, though Conceptual Art did so explicitly. The philosophical bases of art changed, and even the acceptance that art *was* a system signified the tremendous changes underway, opening it not only to critical analysis, but to integrated management theorising and normalisation. In fact, the artists' revolt of the 1960s (which also helped transform the system) opened up quite a few spaces to which artists could repair, withdrawing from the high-end product-oriented, heavily policed system, towards low-cost, easily disseminated forms, such as cheap multiples, photography, and eventually video, and also to develop an apparently uncapitalisable form, 'performance'. Performance permitted artists to intersect with their own perceived community – the art-music-poetry-fiction-theatre-dance-movie crowd – without the otherwise requisite high production values or finished-product orientation, even that of theatrical 'improv' (improvisation).

The art world has, in the interim, managed to sweep into the centre everything it might recuperate from the margins, including graffiti art – anything that might have disruptive force – and repurpose it. This has led post-modernists to say rather smugly that there is no 'outside' (outside society, outside the art world) and that it is romantic to think otherwise. It is hard to argue with this, but it ignores the dimension of time – the pace of unfolding – in which the spaces are opened that allow for new meanings to emerge, before they are dimmed or swallowed up. It also seems to ignore the changing stories that form the contexts of reception, which make old 'utterances' new again.

One should always remind people that they *are* the public. Artists act politically in the public world, both as individuals and as artists. But many are also producing critical and political artworks, whether they acknowledge that or not. Many refuse the embrace of institutional venues and instead work with so-called interventions or tactical media, as you know, and the formation of collectives has gone far towards irritating art lovers of every stripe. But when artists completely give up connections to the art world, they become 'community artists' and are rendered invisible to the art world. Even operating as I did for so many years, without commercial representation, made me virtually invisible, no matter how visible I was to artists and university faculty members – or even how many museum shows I was included in! By the early 1990s, this was no longer a tenable position in fact, as borne out by the change in my apparent status once I joined a gallery in 1993.

For the world, the image of New York City is often everything but Communism. But you lived here through a good part of your life and have seen many faces of the city. What traces of Communism were manifest in New York as you experienced it? Are there any remnants of Communism today?

I am not sure whether to interpret your question to mean Communism with a capital C, or communism as a more diffuse concept, as we have been discussing. The only thing I can offer is a potted history based on presupposition and memory. You are not native New Yorkers, so the history is probably opaque to you, but there are some very good published histories of the New York, and the US, left. In fact, the rest of New York State, and probably most of the United States, sees New York City as the very hotbed of Leftism, and Jewish leftism at that (not the first time that anti-Semitism has been bolstered by anti-communism). New York has had a long and vibrant history of leftism, especially because it was until recently a major port and industrial centre and a feeder of immigrants for much of the rest of the Continental United States. Like nineteenth-century Liverpool, New York is 'cosmopolitan', an international city, and as such has a certain degree of sovereignty, a virtual wall between itself and the rest of the nation, which is decidedly suspicious of it. Like Liverpool, New York has had constantly shifting ethnic, religious, political, cultural, and economic groupings. But unlike Liverpool, it is and has remained a vital centre of international capital. Class, race, and ethnicity by and large determine where people live, and although many neighbour-hoods are segregated racially or ethnically, others are not. In many respects, New York is heterogeneous for the upper middle class and above, the knowledge and financial in-dustry workers, and often segregated for the working class and poor. In poor neighbour-hoods (communities), life follows a classic pattern (see note 10, Tönnies) of small-scale commerce, and relationships are personalised rather than professionalised.

The turn of the twentieth century saw several large, successive waves of immigration, mostly from Eastern and Southern Europe, and these groups brought many different forms of communal and self-help organisations. Earlier waves of immigration in the nineteenth century had been largely Irish and German, and, in smaller numbers, Chinese. There was an African-American population of long standing.[15] As a Jew I am most familiar with Jewish life, and my family – typically for Jewish immigrants – refused to look back, insisting that 'we are Americans now' (this had become especially important because of the literally unspeakable trauma of the Holocaust, since everyone left behind in the Old Country was, my mother assured me, 'dead, all dead'). But that meant that her community was at best dimly related to its origins in part of Europe. Newly arrived European Jews at the turn of the century became garment workers and sought lodging in decrepit, deeply impoverished lower Manhattan; shoddy new tenements were quickly added to accommodate them. The perpetual housing crisis led to new housing laws, and a new tenement design was adopted after an architectural competition. For these new immigrants, aside from religious organisations, there were the necessary burial societies and also Jewish chapters of fraternal lodges (existing ones excluded Jews), like the Masons and Odd Fellows, and the Hadassah for women – several members of my family were affiliated with these – as well as newspapers, cultural societies, and theatre groups.

Religious organisations existed alongside cultural organisations concerned with identity preservation apart from religious commitment, such as furthering Yiddish literary culture, and alongside more political organisations. The early twentieth century was a high point of left-wing organisation in New York and beyond. The parks, such as Union Square and Tompkins Square Park in the Lower East Side, and 125th Street in Harlem (then a largely Italian and Jewish area), were speakers' platforms, much like London's Hyde Park. The US was also periodically convulsed by anti-left (combined with anti-immigrant) campaigns and paranoias, its successive gov-ernments having been frightened by the various European uprisings in the nineteenth century. Anarchist agitation and bombings in various US cities, including the Haymar-ket bombing in Chicago and the assassination of President McKinley by a foreign-born anarchist, led to trials, executions, and deportations. Emma Goldman, for example, who had moved to New York in the late nineteenth century and was agitating on a number of fronts (including labour rights, birth control, and anti-war platforms), was imprisoned and then deported, along with Alexander Berkmann and others. After the war, the Great Red Scare of 1919-1920 led to further round ups and deportations and the 'high-profile' trial and execution of the militant anarchists Nicola Sacco and Bartolomeo Vanzetti in Massachusetts for a crime they did not commit.

Fear of the insurrectionary poor, whether immi-grant or native-born, had spurred the turn-of-the-century Progressive Movement, led by social elites, which took over the Republican Party under Teddy Roosevelt. Progressives created the 'settlement house' and social-work movements in Chicago and New York. Immigrants were greeted by 'Americanisation' campaigns conducted not only by estab-lished co-religionists but by the settlement houses. My mother, born to Russian Jewish immigrants on the Lower East Side, was, from age 8, a member of one such settlement house, Christodora House.[16] The Henry Street Settlement, also on the Lower East Side, continues to serve its surrounding community, whose ethnicity has shifted from Jewish to Latino and Chinese. I think it would be a mistake simply to dismiss the humanitarian motives, reform activities, and affiliations of the settlement house and social-work movements, including founders such as Jane Addams (Chicago) and Lillian Wald (New York). Thirty years later, Franklin Roosevelt's Depression-era administration, which introduced elements of the 'welfare state', operated under a similar presupposition: that conditions urgently needed amelioration if revolution – now potentially including the unemployed middle class – was to be avoided, and by this time, the international communist movement had a base, in the Soviet Union.

The left was internationalised, but in the 1930s, the Communist sector, in the US as in many European countries, soon adopted a strategy of forming a Popular Front with non-Communist allies, allowing the party to avoid having to support a war against the Nazis – until the Soviet Union joined the war against Germany. The left, certainly after the formation of the Soviet Union and its policy shifts, underwent the doctrinal and political schisming I referred to earlier. The inter-war period in New York was one of robust leftist organisation and agitation, much of it labour-related. The garment union, which is still operative (New York was famously the centre of the garment industry, primarily staffed with Jewish immigrants), built modern high-rise housing for their members on the Lower East Side waterfront. There were neighbourhood sports leagues in the boroughs and also participation in avant-garde literature, art, music, and dance; there was a vibrant intellectual culture at the movement's core. The Harlem Renaissance of black intelligentsia of the 1920s and 1930s included a number of people who identified as socialists or communists. Amongst Catholics, the anarchist Catholic Worker, founded by Dorothy Day and Peter Maurin in 1933, was active (and remains so) mostly as a group advocating for the poor in many cities but begun on the Lower East Side. Many anti-capitalist groups, with many different orientations towards the Soviet Union and towards questions of organising, reform, and revolution – Trotskyist, Schachtmanite, communist, Labour Zionist, and others – were on the scene, and many had youth groups. As Vivian Gornick has pointed out, everyone believed that 'revolution was right around the corner' (a millenarian belief, to be sure, but one prompted not only by the October Revolution but by the immiseration caused by the Depression).[17] New York City's free university system, especially at the flagship institution, all-male City College, was home to highly politicised students in the 1930s. A handful of anti-Stalinist, largely Trotskyist, Jewish students went on to found or contribute to highly influential little journals, most prominently *The Partisan Review*. Some of this group, including Irving Kristol, Irving Howe, Nathan Glazer, and Daniel Bell, became Cold War anti-communist liberals. In the 1960s, partly as a result of their support for the Vietnam War, some became early 'neo-conservatives' and war hawks.[18] Other prominent members of the so-called New York Intellectuals (so-called because they dominated the city's intellectual life for decades), all on the left to one or another degree but all anti-Stalinist, included Philip Rahv, William Phillips, Mary McCarthy, Lionel Trilling, Sidney Hook, Dwight Macdonald, and Alfred Kazin, and also Clement Greenberg. Unlike most of these other writers and critics, Greenberg, of course, was an art critic and became the pre-eminent shaper of Abstract Expressionism after the war.

The labour organising and social projects of the left continued through the 1930s and 1940s. New York even elected a socialist city councilman, Vito Marcantonio, on the American Labour Party line. After the Second World War Communist Party membership was outlawed by the federal government and leftists were purged from the union movement (which helped drive some unions into the arms of the criminal mobs) and from many civil positions, including teaching.

Hollywood in 1948 held the first US anti-communist hearings and instituted a blacklist, and many of the writers who were banned were originally New York Jews. The 1950s were the era of McCarthyism, named after the wide-ranging political 'witch hunts' of Wisconsin Senator Joseph McCarthy. It brought about the fall of J. Robert Oppenheimer, the architect of the atomic bomb at Los Alamos in the Second World War's secret Manhattan Project, a fall probably engineered by Oppenheimer's opponent, Edward Teller, who was the proponent first of the 'super' (the hydrogen bomb) and then, in the 1980s, of the idiotic Star Wars defence system, under Ronald Reagan. (Teller actually was the model for Stanley Kubrick's *Dr. Strangelove*.) Oppenheimer was the exemplary left-leaning, Jewish, universalist scientist who may have sympathised with the scientists who demanded that the bomb science and technology be shared with all, including with the Soviets, but he was not on the side of those who, like Klaus Fuchs, Theodore Hall, and others, actually did so.[19] This atom hysteria led to the public trial and eventual execution of the young, quintessentially left-wing – probably with Communist Party membership – Lower East Side New Yorkers, Julius and Ethel Rosenberg. The Rosenberg saga, and their electrocution, haunted my childhood. (In 1988, upon invitation, I produced a work about the Rosenbergs, centred on Ethel and on US nuclear blackmail.) McCarthyism also led to the hounding and firing of many New Yorkers, especially teachers. My mother, a grade-school teacher, scorned any talk of teachers' unions (but when unionisation succeeded in the 1960s she became a fervent supporter), since the destruction of the militantly left (probably Communist-dominated) Teachers Union of the 1930s. The political atmosphere in New York in the 1950s – even for a child like me – was one of nuclear terror, on the one hand, and the terror of the Commie-hunting FBI, on the other. I had several friends whose families lived under pseudonyms, and several others never said much on the phone because wiretapping clicks were periodically audible.

Young hipsters, intellectuals, and artists aspired to join New York's downtown art scene. Bohemianism and folk and blues culture, in San Francisco, New York, Chicago, and other cities, took for granted an entwined cultural and political critique.[20] Beatnik culture was, of course, 'bohemian' rather than leftist, but a left orientation was presumed nonetheless. The Trotskyist Young People's Socialist League seemed to be everywhere, though I never did see any of their literature; but as a teenager I first saw Eisenstein's film *Battleship Potemkin* in a screening they held. Regular cultural events were also sponsored by the Arbeiter Ring (Workmen's Circle), a left-wing group (still active) born of socialist Jewish immigrants; secularist Jews like these were known as Bundists, after the socialist Jewish Labour Bund, a mass organisation in Lithuania, Poland, and czarist Russia in the late nineteenth century. Friday nights I attended free concerts by some of the most internationally important musical groups, at a Manhattan high school under the aegis of some populist organisation or other. Proselytising was low to nonexistent at most of these events; their existence alone, I suppose, was intended as the calling card. Other groups held public lectures and ran informal schools, on the model of the turn-of-the-century union movements; today's Brecht Forum is an outgrowth of the Marxist School that was founded in the 1960s or 1970s. In high school I joined anti-nuclear protests defying duck-and-cover air-raid drills, which was illegal at the time; we students also circulated postcard petitions for the Congress of Racial Equality, although 'Don't sign anything!' was our parents' watchword, for dissent or an arrest could mean a lifetime without gainful employment.

Brooklyn College, the free city school I attended (at the time probably over 90% Jewish) had been politically purged in the 1950s, but the campus, like others, was undergoing re-politicisation in response to the civil rights and student movements, and in defence of the new Cuban revolution – not to mention rage over the Cuban missile crisis, which we literally thought would end our lives. The civil rights movement and its successors provided the first great awakening. Students joined SNCC on the 'freedom rides' to register black voters in the South. I attended a classroom debate with Malcolm X, where the crowd, typically, filled the hallways, and I drove down to join the March on Washington with friends in 1963. Meeting after meeting was held to discuss political positions and strategies, a new thing for most of us. By the mid-1960s we were holding student strikes, 'teach ins', and sit-ins there. But the issue of the war itself, because of the de-politicisation of the 1950s, was not a direct focus of on-campus demands until a bit later (demands centred on the status of students as self-determining adults and, as in the Berkeley origins of the student movement, on the relationship between bureaucracy, loss of individuality, and the 'war machine'). The student strike leaders (including my husband-to-be) were inevitably red baited, and the college president – also the head of the liberal anti-communist Freedom House – quoted the old saw to the effect that if it walked and talked like a duck, it must be a duck, meaning we were all crypto-communists. Even *The New York Times* editorialised against us. But too late!

Through these movements, and the rise of the New Left, a horde of young people rediscovered the entire spectrum of the left, including the 'Old Left' of the 1930s, a connection that had effectively been severed by McCarthyism. The post-war 'baby boom' meant that the majority of the population was younger than 25. The Old Left may have been sure the revolution was just around the corner; the younger generation instead lived under the cloud of a nuclear apocalypse. Chapters of Students for a Democratic Society (SDS) formed all over the country. The Columbia University strike of 1967 – an anti-war sit-in at New York's Ivy League school, the second oldest university in the nation – was an earth-shaking event. Huge antiwar marches were held regularly in New York. President Johnson's administration was sure the 'Movement' was communist 'infiltrated,' but the fact is, it simply was not; organised Old Left groups were a tiny minority amongst the antiwar activists.

A flood of literature was translated from mostly German sources in the late 1960s, including the *Kulturkritik* of Herbert Marcuse and the Frankfurt School. By then, I had become a Californian. Inadvertently, by joining a generation of young city dwellers setting out for adventure, I also participated in white flight (though I expected to return, and I did). Partly as a result of repression, as well as questions of leadership, the black movement split into non-violent and militant wings, and there were riots and uprisings in several cities, notably Detroit and Newark, and nationwide, after the assassination of Martin Luther King Jr., in 1968. Whites openly expressed fear of insurrection, while amongst the things worrying the government was that in both Detroit and Newark, if not elsewhere, black insurrectionists were joined by poor whites. The Black Panther Party was formed in this moment, as well as the American Indian Movement, the Chicano movement, the women's liberation movement, and the gay liberation movement, The left, essentially the entire antiwar movement, was also dividing over tactical and doctrinal issues, and in 1969 SDS was a casualty. Many turned to Maoism, and other forms of 'Third Worldism', and tactically a small number wanted to engage in provocations like bombing military and other government facilities, to bypass even vanguardist self-organisation in favour of the hoped-for uprisings in the face of stepped-up repression. The Weather Underground

(Weatherman) was formed, probably in New York; in Manhattan's West Village several of their novice bomb makers blew themselves up in an expensive townhouse in 1970. Downtown Brooklyn's military recruitment station was bombed by persons unknown. A Puerto Rican separatist group bombed historic Fraunces Tavern on Wall Street (and in the 1980s bombed the Brooklyn Federal Courthouse on New Year's Eve). All these bombings were intended to damage property, not people, although there were casualties – including the broad antiwar, 'anti-imperialist' consensus.

In New York, as the middle class (both black and white) left the city for the suburbs, and the extensive manufacturing sector left for overseas, political organising continued in 'communities of colour', especially black, Latino, and Chinese (the use of the term 'communities' as we have established, indicating poverty and isolation). Throughout the 1970s, and the late 1980s New York organising was dominated by poor people's movements. The groups were mostly centred on self-help as well as public assistance and housing, such as the squatter/sweat-equity movements in the sections of Manhattan left to founder through malign neglect. Groups such as the Black United Front and Harlem Fight Back formed to show a militant face in their demands for city services and against police brutality; these political groups were more defensive than programmatic, as city services – including firehouses – were withdrawn to produce what one city bureaucrat termed 'planned shrinkage'; but forcing people to move destroys communities and damages their members. The Bronx and the Lower East Side burned as landlords torched their buildings for the insurance. No one was prosecuted, but these areas fell to ruin – and long-term financial speculation. Yippies and hippies joined Latino community activists to try to save the Lower East Side for its poor residents (including artists, writers, and bohemian counter-culturalists in general).

There was in this period a panoply of leftish cults, some focused on self-help and therapy; but unlike out West, where such cults as EST and even the politically progressive 'Re-evaluation counselling' (or 'co-counselling'), were focused on the small art community and other middle-class 'affinity groups', the pernicious New York versions settled amongst the poor communities of colour, where at least one resides to this day, in the guise of a political party and an art centre – for 'community' arts.[21] Scientology (which doesn't have an enormous foothold in New York) is similar but with nothing resembling a 'progressive' collectivism.

Although I can't continue this discussion here, it is important to note that one of the discoveries of the New Left, which thought it was avoiding the bureaucratic centralism of the Old Left through participatory democracy and a temporary suspension of political 'lines', was that the micro-politics of communities were beyond their grasp. What I mean is that groups that profess egalitarianism generally wind up with unacknowledged leaders who lead by other means, which often amounts to manipulation and even intra-group shaming of dissidents. Such group dynamics can be met with control techniques, as feminists and others discovered. The communes of the 1960s and 1970s, where some of my Brooklyn friends decamped in the 'back to the land' movements and some of which I visited when I lived out West, tried to use neo-primitivism to escape urban ills. The effectively anti-modern movements wanted to adopt tribal forms of association much like what one might call the Iroquois ideal of direct democracy. Some perhaps succeeded, but others, I speculate – especially those not interested or engaged in left-wing self-education, but with other goals in mind, including the rise of New Age spiritualism ('turn on, tune in, drop out', to borrow Timothy Leary's phrase) – accepted a redefined gender inequality and types of leadership that much of the left was no longer willing to do.[22]

Although the Communist Party (CPUSA) was careful to include people of colour and women, by the 1960s the growing influence of 'nationalist' identities in movements of people of colour, such as the Black Panthers and the Black Power movement (based primarily outside New York), and the West's Chicano movement, and of course the rise of feminism, meant that the self-identified left was increasingly white, though the women, especially white women of the New Left, did not fully desert the left movements.[23] Socialist feminism was the dominant strain of non-essentialist feminism. Environmentalism produced some disaffection and splitting with the left, because the received versions of Marxism that privileged the industrial proletariat seemed to take for granted the continuing ethos of domination of nature that characterises industrialisation.

In 1970s' New York, the desperate efforts of the power elites were directed towards returning the city to fiscal stability, for the crashing of the tax base had produced an unprecedented fiscal crisis that led to receivership under a city/state corporation led by the finance banker Felix Rohatyn. Their concerted efforts to drive the poor out of Manhattan and establish it as a centre of the 'FIRE' industries (finance, insurance, and real estate) – in other words, as a financial centre above all, and a pre-eminent one – was accompanied by a campaign to scapegoat and break the municipal unions, on the one hand, and on the other, to reduce the number of people drawing public assistance. The art scene had remained, of course, but contemporary-art dealers were not doing particularly well. The art scene had many self-organised, artist-run galleries (or 'spaces'), and the growing East Village scene led to the formation of new commercial dealerships there. The eventual success of the city and state's bureaucratic manoeuvres came at the end of the 1970s, at the same time that the commercial art world found its next big thing, the commodification of new forms (performance and, much later, video) and big neo-(neo) Expressionist, paintings, beginning with those imported from Germany and Italy, thus for the first time in the post-war period showcasing European artists.

The early 1980s saw, for the first time, the privileging of the work of very young artists in commercial galleries, whose purchase was presumed to be equivalent to getting in on the ground floor of a new trend. The rest is history – international history. It took a while, but the independent artist-run scene (greatly potentiated by the National Endowment for the Arts, begun in the late 1960s, and a rather wonderful program called CETA, instituted by Jimmy Carter and immediately cancelled by Ronald Reagan, which subsidised young staff members at cultural and community institutions) was marginalised.

The late 1970s brought the return to the cities of the middle class (the sector newly named yuppies, or young urban professionals), who renovated old or disused buildings and took over poor districts, a process for which the word 'gentrification' was invented. That process went hand in hand with the invention of artists' districts, which began with lower Manhattan's rapidly emptying small-manufacturing area, now called SoHo, or South of Houston, in the late 1960s (the same area that was supposed to have been effectively destroyed by a highway running through it, the last project of the urban-planning demiurge Robert Moses, but which was prevented by the public campaigning of Jane Jacobs and her neighbours arguing for neighbourhood-as-community).[24] This powerful paradigm, in which 'certified' artists could renovate and live legally in lofts (they had been unofficially doing so in many cities for many years) – and then possibly buy them – gave the district cachet, which led to high prices on resale in the 1980s and the eventual end of artists' residency in such districts. *New York Magazine* celebrated and promoted 'loft living,' rendering it visible and desirable to the world, making it unnecessary to turn loft districts into artist districts before selling them to yuppies and others.

The 1990s saw a type of practice that drew upon a kind of community participation – the art world was the presumed community in question – marking a departure from previous notions of artists serving communities, which was a long-standing feature of the left for many years and had resurfaced in the 1970s with, say, Chicano Arts projects and Judy Baca's Sparc in East Los Angeles and other projects in San Francisco, San Diego, Chicago, and elsewhere – and with the Women's Building in Los Angeles, intending to serve the broad community of women artists. Michael Zinzun ran youth video workshops in Los Angeles, on which artist Nancy Buchanan also collaborated for a time. By the 1980s and 1990s, there were public art projects run by groups like Group Material and a spin off, Tim Rollins's K.O.S., or Kids of Survival project in the devastated South Bronx; Wendy Ewald's work with poor, rural children in several countries; Dona McAdams's work with farmers and other residents in West Virginia; Daoud Bey's collaborative photo project with poor urban, mostly African American and Latino teenagers; and many more. Some of these projects benefited from public funding. Some bureaucrats in more than a few cities desired such a project, to 'manage diversity'.

But in more recent years, a different, far more visible group of practices has emerged, sometimes likened to a 'gift economy', following the terminology of anthropologists such as Marcel Mauss, most of them falling under the rubric of 'relational aesthetics'. These projects cannot help but treat the art world as their community and quite possibly see their public/audience/participants as microcosmic laboratories for wider change. They are often specifically anti-ideological, however.[25] This is not my vision.

How does your library project fit into the questions of community, as we have been exploring them?

I'm of the opinion that a utopian horizon is necessary, though I would not describe myself as a utopian. The library project, which began as the suggestion of Anton Vidokle at e-flux and is an e-flux project on which we are collaborators, should not be seen as allied with these other projects, any more than should the various 'garage sales' that I have held in art world institutions; I prefer to emphasise criticality and information exchange, and the need for social transformation, despite the literal existence of 'exchanges' between participants. Anton Vidokle refers to the library as an act of generosity, but for some in the mainstream art world it seems to represent 'a portrait of the artist', which as one might imagine interests me the least. What engaged me was the possibility of affirming the depth and breadth of the discourses that go into the making of an artist. I wanted to counter the finally superficial ideas of genius (deep) or cleverness (fashionable talent) that pervade magazine articles and museum press releases. With this project, of close to 8,000 books on many subjects, I am indeed speaking to, and of, the art community, as an open-ended and discontinuous and episodic one – the library represents the community of ideas, of which, as I suggested, art partakes. The library has also occasioned reading groups (a time-honoured artists' activity) and related screenings and public events, here in New York where it spent six months at e-flux's tiny storefront gallery and at the Frankfurter Kunstverein, and presumably will do so during its time at MuHKA in Antwerp and then in Berlin, where Vidokle has been in essence reconstituting the school department of Manifesta 6 that recently fell to politics. Ideally, the library (it is more properly a reading room, since one cannot borrow books), as it was in New York, is situated alongside other stores, services, and attractions.

I have done other projects relating to community, such as *If You Lived Here…*, at New York's Dia Art Foundation in 1989, for which 'Housing Is a Human Right' was the unofficial motto. Fifty artists and groups – artists and activists, squatters and advocates, film-makers and architects, poets and planners – contributed to a cycle of three shows and four public forums on the past, present, and future of housing. My project at Utopia Station in the Venice Biennale of 2003 engaged several disparate groups of students and artists in various cities and countries in dreaming up a cross-border ideal state and contributing to a rethinking of utopia.

Your photo and video retrospective at the Sprengel Museum in Hanover in 2005 was entitled If Not Now, When? *and your website proclaims it as well. Does that have meaning in the context of this discussion?*

This is part of a saying of the early, foundational Jewish sage Hillel, who lived in Jerusalem under Herod.

'If I am not for me, who is for me? If I am only for me, who am I? And if not now, when?'

It goes to the heart of the basic Jewish idea of communalism, including the doctrine of 'Tikkun Olam': He who saves one person rescues the world. I won't go into the way this is or is not typical of all religious movements. But when prompted, long ago, by America Online to choose a motto for my profile (part of the fake community of AOL-users that such corporate entities were trying to develop at the time), I chose 'If not now, when'. When my son, Joshua Neufeld, established a website for me as a birthday present, he saw it there and picked up the motto for the site. For Hanover, the curator Inka Schube, in turn, saw it on my site and chose it for the show. 'If not now, when?' seemed an appropriate motto for those interested in activism, which must be timely and engaged. Its link to the larger question of self, community, and responsibility, however, is what makes it come alive.

NOTES.

1. See Jürgen Habermas's *Structural Transformation of the Public Sphere*, 1962, but also his short encyclopaedia article, translated as 'The Public Sphere' in Armand Mattelart & Seth Siegelaub (Eds.), *Communication and Class Struggle*, International General, New York, 1979, and in Stephen Eric Bronner and Douglas Kellner,(Eds.), *Critical Theory and Society, A Reader*, Routledge, New York, 1989.

2. I would imagine that council communism and other visions of communal rule intended to install agency at the site of relatively small, often work-based units, rather than in a central supreme governing council or individual.

3. Hannah Arendt, *On Violence*, Harcourt Brace Jovanovich, New York, 1969, pp. 81-82.

4. Hannah Arendt, *The Origins of Totalitarianism*, Meridian Books, 1958, p. 263.

5. Not all religious movements hold maximalist goals, but it is important to note that theocracies do not recognise the idea of civil society as a neutral space not *ipso facto* governed by religious law. Some version of this argument was behind the banning of communist parties in the US and elsewhere: because these parties were held to support the overthrow of the legitimate government (whether they did so or not) and the institution of a 'dictatorship of the proletariat' (again, a charge that would need considerable explanation), they could not be allowed to participate in the political process.

6. In this unity government the new Kadima Party formed a coalition with its main rival, Labour and immediately co-opted the Labour party's dovish head, a union leader, into the defence rather than the finance ministry, thus ending his hopes of aiding the declining condition of working-class wage earners and putting him into the group spear- heading the disastrous war in Lebanon. Hamas, to get their funds unfrozen, also may agree to a unity government with its bitter rival, the secular Fatah (founded by Yassir Arafat), which controls the premiership.

7. Retort (Iain Boal, T.J. Clark, Joseph Matthews, Michael Watts), *Afflicted Powers: Capital and Spectacle in a New Age of War*, Verso, London and New York, 2005.

8. Nancy is attempting to formulate a notion of community which would never congeal into a one; community for him is also an act of unworking. In English his text has been translated as the inoperative community, but it could also be read as the unworked, even unworking community. It basically argues for an understanding of community that is in some sense negative, or sees in community not only a move towards the common, but also a subtraction from anything that would become one, a purely unified or closed body.

9. Benedict Anderson, *Imagined Communities: Reflections on the Origin and Spread of Nationalism*, Verso, London and New York,1983.

Anderson writes: 'In an anthropological spirit… I propose the following definition of the nation: it is an imagined political community – and imagined as both inherently limited and sovereign' (p. 5).

10. Because the term seems to incorporate pre-urban or small-town shared values. This is reflected in the use of the term by the early sociologist Ferdinand Tönnies in his classic work *Gemeinschaft und Gessellschaft* 1887; (translated into English as *Community and Society*). The book, reflecting a moment in which that small-town consensus of social bonds formed by proximity and 'face-to-face' relations is being superseded by an urbanised, corporate society, sees communities as, at base, associations held together by affective as opposed to instrumental bonds.

11. Brian Holmes, 'Network, Swarm, Microstructure', in *Multitudes* online (May 2006). In this essay, Holmes adopts the formulations of sociologist Karin Knorr Cetina to outline the contemporary ways in which people organise themselves but also refers to the history of these ideas over four decades.

12. James Cuno (Ed.), *Whose Muse? Art Museums and the Public Trust*, Princeton University Press, Princeton, 2003. Also see, for example, Chin-tao Wu's *Privatising Culture: Corporate Art Intervention since the 1980s*, Verso, London, 2002, especially her discussion of 'enterprise culture.'

13. Or, alternatively, *House Beautiful: Bringing the War Home*; in this context, the order of title and subtitle does not matter very much, and in the past I have used either.

14. In the early 1990s I allowed the earlier series of works to be shown in museums and galleries, where I considered them 'not themselves but representative of themselves', partly to preserve the historical record – that such works had been done – and partly to attach them to my own name. Now, the Guggenheim and the Met, as well as MoMA and the V&A, and other institutions, and individuals, own or exhibit images from this series. This preserves a historical record of artist criticality; beyond that, I don't know.

15. New York had, of course, been a slave-holding area, and there were also several communities of free blacks. New York's worst riots, the Civil War draft riots of 1863, centred on the resistance of Irish immigrants to joining the army but the mob soon turned on Republicans and the city's black residents, a number of whom were murdered.

16. At Christodora, my mother gained an appreciation and awe of European art and culture, especially British culture, but as an adult she never visited museums or any foreign country but Israel, remaining completely embedded in Jewish culture. She never regarded her experience as clashing allegiances but only as part of becoming American (she drew a line, however, at 'church music,' such as Bach's). Her club of neighbourhood girls, formed at Christodora, lasted most of her long

life, long after Christodora was closed and its building was converted into condominiums.

17. Vivian Gornick, *The Romance of American Communism*, Basic Books, New York, 1977.

18. Irving Howe remained a democratic socialist, but he was a hawk on the Vietnam War. Neither Bell nor Glazer can be quite so easily categorised. Again, this is not the appropriate place to discuss this, but the term 'neo-conservative' is meant to distinguish those who are socially conservative but in favour of a strong national security state from older, or 'paleo'-conservatives who desire to limit government power. This clique is so much in the ascendancy that almost all right-wingers are popularly referred to in the US as 'neo-cons'.

19. Like so many of the scientists of that era, Teller also was Jewish, born in Hungary.

20. All the more so after the US embraced Abstract Expressionism as ambassador of American freedom in the 1950s and covertly financed, through the CIA, a few small but influential, apparently leftist, literary journals, a fact that, when it emerged in the late 1960s, caused much hand-wringing and embarrassment.

21. Lenore Fulani and her mentor, Fred Newman of the New Alliance Party (with their even more cult-like International Workers Party and Social Therapy groups behind it) is the most prominent representative in New York politics of this version of political vanguardism (a type of Leninism). These groups were derived from therapy groups with progressive politics – amongst them the Sullivanians, based on the writings of Harry Stack Sullivan. Their goal was, like the co-counseling movement, to help individuals (re)gain the ability to wield collective power without succumbing to authoritarian leadership. The opposite seems to have occurred in the case of the New York group.

22. A commonly heard debate which produced a major set of alignments was over what to attempt to change first: society or oneself. Some of the therapy groups, obviously – including women's consciousness-raising groups, a central core of feminism of that era – sought to answer: both!

23. Angela Davis, a philosophy student of Herbert Marcuse at the University of California, San Diego (I too was studying there and attending Marcuse lectures and knew both Angela and her sister Fania, both activists), joined the Communist Party in the early 1970s.

24. I don't believe this was a strategy that could foresee the course it would follow, described below.

25. They bring to mind the way some artists have adopted the model of 'heterotopia' from Michel Foucault: exploiting the interstices of modern urban societies, existing in the cracks of society, without quite challenging the social order.

MERV BRAZINSKI PRESENTS

THE THREE FAILURES

A FAIRY TALE ABOUT COMMUNISM, SOCIAL-DEMOCRACY AND CAPITALISM
FEATURING MIKHAIL & SERGEI M. EISENSTEIN – ISAIAH BERLIN – IRVING BERLIN
WINSTON & LADY CHURCHILL – RICHARD WAGNER – ADAM SMITH AND MORE
PRODUCED BY MERV BRAZINSKI – WRITTEN, DIRECTED & PERFORMED BY MICHAEL BLUM

THE THREE FAILURES:
VOICE-OVER
Michael Blum

On 23 January, 1898, Mikhail Eisenstein, a well-established architect in the city of Riga, was given a son. It's this very baby who, 29 years later, was to become the first person to conceive a film of Marx's *Capital*, after a script by Marx himself. It is still unknown up to this day whether the extreme low temperature of this night in January 1898, one of the coldest in the whole century, had any bearing on Eisenstein's failure thirty years later. Anyway, Eisenstein's *Notes for a Film of Capital*, now published, show that filming *Capital* was not just a vague idea pulled out of a magician's hat during a vodka-marathon. It was a project carefully considered, intensively discussed, partially researched and tentatively planned. Seeking a way to make the viewer think dialectically (that's why Deleuze nicknamed him 'the cinematographic Hegel'), Eisenstein was focusing on the worker and the bowl of soup prepared by his wife while he was producing capital at the factory. For Eisenstein, the worker's wife was one of the major threats to the revolution, since she was preventing him from being hungry – and therefore revolutionary. Today, things have dramatically shifted. The angels of Capitalism have figured out great ways to feed our stomachs and brains in order to keep us quiet. The central political issue of the day is not 'what should be done?' anymore, but 'where can I find a fitness club that accepts my credit card?'

Despite the efforts and ideas on how to adapt Marx's script, Eisenstein's project failed, both because *Capital* was simply too much of a subject and because Stalin had decided to stop the smart young man. This initial failure, for whatever reason, might have triggered a whole series of failures, throughout the world and the century – and even beyond.

First, Communism didn't last too long. 72 years, that's what it took for Communism to fail – or rather the wall to fall. From Bishkek to Sofia, the experience of defeat has become the only horizon and the bowl of soup is back on the worker's table. In the end, alienation in spite of liberation was not the solution. The spectre might still be roaming around but we, proud individuals and capitalist subjects, are not afraid of ghosts, are we? Even if Communism didn't really fail, but was rather abused by a drunken husband, the idea of its failure has been made so irresistible that no one can seriously oppose it.

Then: Social Democracy, or the quasi-utopian programme outlined in Sweden in the 1930s and applied to Scandinavian countries, seemed to offer a better product for a cheaper price. The great modernist project, which experienced so many difficulties under totalitarian regimes, was here fully and successfully applied. The state managed to get rid of poverty and to become one of the world's wealthiest. To achieve this miracle, the state had to sneak into any aspect of both public and private lives – organising, rewarding, punishing and ruling in a general consent. Yet the social order that characterised Swedish life ended up being quite repressive. The individual was strangled and suffocated for the sake of social comfort and in the name of a better tomorrow. It's even surprising that Sweden, with its soft yet constant, thorough and efficient repression, never produced any violent nutcases like Jack the Ripper, Baruch Goldstein or Marc Dutroux.

At this point, Social Democracy is failing as well. In Sweden as in any other country in the world, it's been smashed by the steamroller of global Capitalism – get rich or get lost. Social Democracy is dissolving in the wake of global Capitalism, for it is hard to resist the logic of accumulation of capital and to lose the sense of one's very private interest. If you're not convinced, just look at the laundry situation in Sweden. Instead of having a washing machine in each apartment, the state ruled that there would be a common laundry room in each building and that the tenants would simply book a time slot. Sounds great, doesn't it? But a few decades later, fights over the laundry facility have become daily business and that's probably the only thing that might make a Swede lose his temper and unpack the machine-gun. The common facility has become a mere battlefield and you'd better enter in full combat gear.

The same happens if you look at the gardens, which used to be communal, without separation between public and private space. Today, fences have been erected in order to mark private property and the open, progressive architecture that constitutes the Swedish suburbs is denied in its essence. Even the idea of the garden has been corrupted, as the worst housing projects in Sweden bear names like Rose Garden, Apple Garden and Cherry Hill, revealing the powerlessness of the social-democratic ideal.

Today, Utopia's remnants are made available worldwide by IKEA, the multi-million-dollar company that is still 100% controlled by the rich landowner's son and former Nazi Ingvar Kamprad. In the end, it's just a matter of time; in principle, the system is already gone.

The only hope left is to be found far away from Sweden, namely in South Africa. During the years of Apartheid, Swedish Social-Democracy was the major role model for non-communist ANC members. Many of them considered the Swedish system fit to be implemented after the fall of Apartheid. Sweden was the biggest and most efficient supporter of the ANC, to the point that South African intelligence services had to get rid of Olof Palme, and with him of a certain idea of Social Democracy. Now, the guys who planned the Olof Palme killing are desperate mercenaries in Congo and Iraq, while their ex-future victims are ruling South Africa. And all enjoy IKEA furniture and its affordable version of the modernist dream.

Victorious Capitalism is now unchallenged and full of itself, parading like an arrogant peacock in a brand-new suit. And it can never call it a day and rest on its achievements, it has to expand ceaselessly, like a restless workaholic. Lenin's apartment in Moscow is now a gift shop and Eisenstein's birth house in Riga could become a Burger King. We wear H&M and Nike, eat McDonald's, drink Coca-Cola, watch CNN, furnish with IKEA, fly Easyjet, enjoy Prozac and don't smoke Marlboros anymore. We are free people in a free world, enjoy a free market and free time. Freedom is awesome.

Yet we know that Capitalism will fail as well – it will smash, crash, and eventually turn *kaput*. Soon, the ruins of Capitalism will join the wreckage of Communism in the post-utopian cemetery of failed political systems. You might argue that Capitalism can't fail. Right. But hasn't Capitalism already failed for 90% of the world's population? So the failure we're looking at here is the final failure, the last quake, the cherry on the cake. And we will not be able to say that we've been taken by surprise. Adam Smith, the early promoter of free trade, had warned us about the deep contradictions inherent to Capitalism – which might lead to an ultimate crisis – but no one paid attention up to yesterday, preferring the comforting sound of his praise of Capitalism. Even Hegel, in his *Philosophy of Right*, was closely following Adam Smith, whilst summing up these contradictions in famous formulas, saying it was 'a world of both great wealth and great poverty'.

So one day – perhaps tomorrow, who knows? – stocks will dramatically drop, a panic attack will hit the city, planes will be grounded, communications will be cut, gas stations and supermarkets will be looted, billionaires will become homeless, prison gates will be opened, car bombs will blow up, the emergency state will be declared, the National Guard will be called in, Afghanistan and Sri Lanka will offer their support, the financial district will become the deadly playground of rats and gangs, there will be no items left to buy or sell. Even the fitness clubs will be shut down. In other words: the dialectics of History in action. Probably a great script idea if Eisenstein was still amongst us…

In the house adjoining Eisenstein's birth house in Riga, Isaiah Berlin was born. The upcoming political philosopher and historian of ideas emigrated to Britain in 1921, the year Mikhail Eisenstein passed away. Isaiah Berlin didn't exactly become a communist, as you can figure out. He was once confused with Irving Berlin, the American composer who probably had a slightly lower IQ than Isaiah Berlin. Winston Churchill invited the latter for lunch, thinking he was the former. So Isaiah Berlin wasn't there, since he was replaced by Irving Berlin, whose real name was actually not even Irving Berlin but Israel Baline, an émigré from Tzarist Russia who made it from the Lower East Side gutter to the Upper East Side condo, writing plenty of songs without knowing how to play the piano or how to read music. He employed arrangers to transcribe the pulsing melodies and often complex harmonies that poured out of his head and through his clumsy fingers. This said, he wrote some of the most famous tunes ever, like *White Christmas* or *God Bless America*. As the titles suggest, he was not exactly driven by a progressive force. A hardcore conservative and lifelong Republican, he gave to a lot of war charities, hence Lady Churchill's desire to thank him, while Winston thought he was having lunch with the other one.

Harry Warren, an Italian-born song-plugger who became Hollywood's top song-maker, said of Irving Berlin in 1944, during the Allied air assault on Germany: 'They bombed the wrong Berlin'.

This brings us back to the infamous London lunch, which took place just before the Allied bombs and Warren's comment, when one Berlin was taken for another.

> Mrs. Churchill said to Winston:
> 'Irving Berlin is in town, he has been very generous to us,
> If you meet him, do tell him we are very pleased with him.'
> Mr. Churchill said,
> 'I want him to come to lunch.'
> She said,
> 'No, no, no, I did not mean that. I mean, if you meet him in the Churchill Club, just pat him on the shoulder and say we are very grateful to him.'
> 'I want him to come to lunch,' he said, but she couldn't understand why.
> So, Irving Berlin sat next to Winston Churchill, who said to him,
> 'Mr. Berlin, what is the most important piece of work you have done for us lately, in your opinion?'
> Poor Berlin obviously couldn't quite make out what this man had said. After some hesitation,
> 'I don't know, it should be *A White Christmas*, I guess.'
> And Winston Churchill said

'Are you an American?'
Berlin said,
'What? Why? Why? Yes.'
Then Churchill again turned to Irving Berlin and he said,
'Do you think Roosevelt will be re-elected this year?'
Irving said,
'Well, in the past I have voted for him myself, this year I
am not so sure.'
At this point, Churchill became rather gloomy, he
couldn't understand who he was dealing with. He
obviously still thought it was Isaiah Berlin, the political
philosopher. Finally, he said,
'Mr. Berlin, when do you think the European War is going
to end?'
Berlin said,
'Sir, I shall never forget this moment. When I go back
to my own country I shall tell my children and my
children's children that in the spring of 1944, the Prime
Minister of Great Britain asked me when the European
War was going to end.'
Churchill was very displeased about this: he really more
or less lost his temper and got up. Lunch was over.

27 years before, another Berlin was the city where Eisenstein's parents moved to after the Revolution. It looked like an obvious choice for upper-class German-speaking Latvians who were unable to accept the October revolution. Even Richard Wagner, the most Germanic of all German composers, has had his time in Latvia. He spent almost two years in Riga between 1837 and 1839 and was the musical director of the Riga German Theatre. According to legend, he found the inspiration for *The Flying Dutchman* on the stormy Baltic Sea when he was leaving Riga, in a depressed state of mind due to unpaid debts.

Latvia has had a few hours of independence, between 1918 and 1940, and again since 1991. Yet, they are like dots in a broad landscape – hardly distinguishable on the Braudelian long-term timeline of History. Once nicknamed the 'Paris of the North', Riga could sooner be dubbed 'Nanook-Vienna'. But does it really matter? Paris and Vienna are the two cities which had their climax roughly between Eisenstein's and Isaiah Berlin's births, and never quite recovered from their past glory. Today, they can only sell the crumbs of their empire as a cultural commodity and offer a disneyfied version of their *grandeur* to the visitor.

By the way, Israel Baline, who became Irving Berlin thanks to the mistake of a record cover printer and not the unleashed imagination of a zealous Ellis Island immigration officer, was NOT born in Riga but in a remote town in Siberia. He set foot on American soil in the years when Capitalism still meant the promise of a golden future – easily reachable for hard workers and lucky folks. If Baline were to emigrate today, he would probably die frozen in the line in front of the US consulate in Wladiwostock. But if the rewards of Capitalism have dramatically shrunk, its promises remain obviously unchanged. Global Capitalism feeds the people, it's the eighth wonder of the world, a light onto the nations, and the answer to everybody's prayers. What is great about America is the greatness of its Gross National Product.

Yet seduction is a matter of illusion. The Bible has replaced the Constitution and War on Terror has taken the place of Struggle for Liberty.

Barbarism in Washington doesn't dress itself in the costumes of Al-Qaeda; it wears instead the smooth-shaven smile of a Senate Resolution sold to the highest bidder. Yet the failure of American Democracy – or Democracy in America – had been announced at least a century and a half ago, by Tocqueville, the compulsory reference of all American presidents since Eisenhower, who quote him constantly without spending too much time reading him. Self-interest well understood, Tocqueville argued, is the moral doctrine best suited to the needs of modern democratic life. Of course, we could update Tocqueville's statement: Ruthless self-promotion is the moral doctrine best suited to the needs of the global market. Benjamin Franklin, one hundred years before, was saying nothing different, distinguishing greed as the main drive of Capitalism. Even Charles Dickens, in his *American Notes for a General Circulation*, saw nothing but the overall failure of the very modern utopia promised by America and its institutions – he saw the third failure outlined already long before we were born.

As a matter of fact, Isaiah Berlin's famous lecture from 1958 entitled 'Two Concepts Of Liberty' should become compulsory reading in Washington. It would show our rulers, if they manage to read it, that they find themselves dealing with a 'negative liberty', the kind of constraint free idleness which leads straight to disaster.

Was it the free market that hijacked the airplanes and promoted them into postmodern bombs? Was it Adam Smith's invisible hand that cut the throats of the pilots on what they thought was a flight to Los Angeles? History apparently is still a work in progress, carrying the promise of the Future Crash, the Grand Failure, the major crack in the world's narrative.

Maybe we have to become utopian idealists again, like our great-grandparents, and harbour the conviction that what is unrealised is better than what is real or even than what is possible. Charles Fourier might not have had his last word yet, maybe he was not fifty years ahead of his time but two-hundred... leaving it up to our children and grandchildren to realise the utopian lifestyle defined in the wake of the Industrial Revolution. At this point, maybe it's time to exit the building, and leave the premises... We need some fresh air. If you find your way out, please let us know. But don't call us, we'll call you. Was a pleasure having you here, have a nice day.

Script from the video work, The Three Failures, *2006*

Sources: Hannah Arendt, Terry Bell, Isaiah Berlin, Mike Bode & Staffan Schmidt, Richard Corliss, Gilles Deleuze, Don DeLillo, Charles Dickens, Sergei M. Eisenstein, Charles Esche & Pavel Büchler, Charles Fourier, Georg Wilhelm Hegel, Christopher Hill, Fredric Jameson, Lewis H. Lapham, Nelson Mandela, Henning Mankell, Herbert Marcuse, Karl Marx, Annette Michelson, Gunnar Myrdal, Jean-Michel Palmier, Gertrud Sandqvist, Charity Scribner, Adam Smith, Alexis de Tocqueville, Max Weber, and Slavoj Žižeck

Fragments from a Communist Latento*
Raqs Media Collective

*A Latento, meaning an elaboration of that which is
latent or hidden, is the antonym of a manifesto, an
assertion of that which is clearly evident

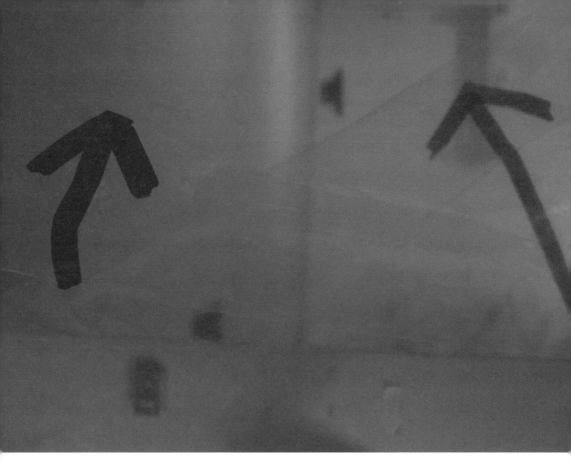

I

The spectre of abundance haunts the empire of scarcity.

Who can ration breath, laughter, thought, desire or madness?

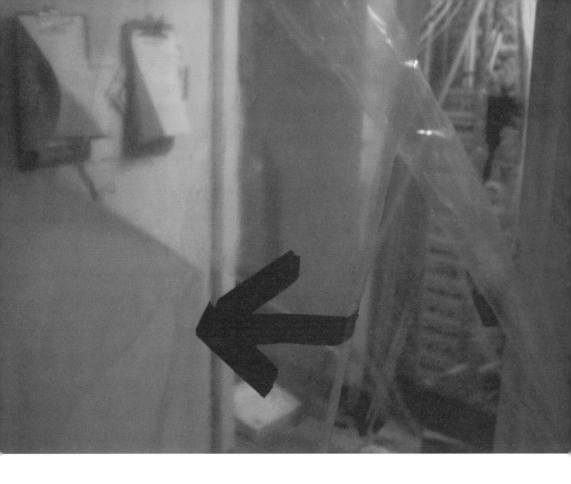

II

It is not desirable that the future be captive to the present.

Just as it is unthinkable that the present be held hostage by the future.

Neither the arrow nor the boomerang of time!

III
A million ways to make things rough is better
than one way to make things smooth.
From each according to their generosity,
to each according to their pleasure

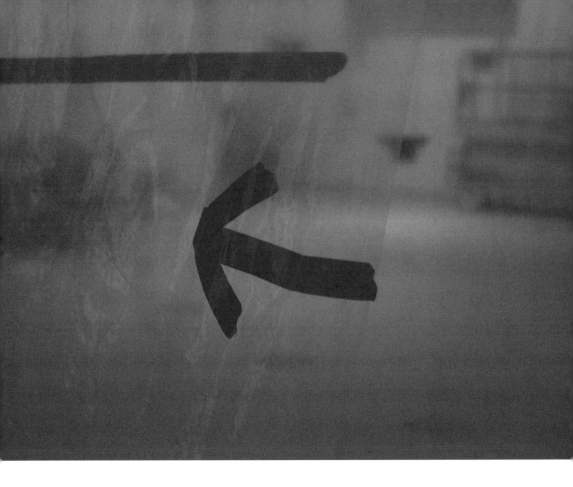

IV

The diversity of the commons challenges the singularity of property.
There is only one way to possess something,
but there can be countless ways to share it.

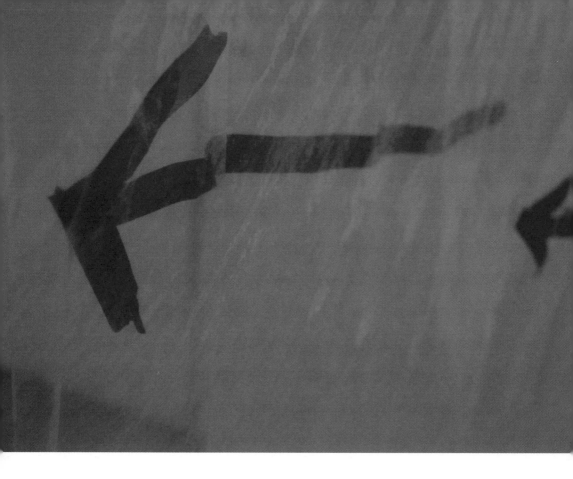

V

We will wait for the time when the socially necessary labour time
to make something can be debated socially.
Until then restlessness will remain the best antidote to exhaustion

VI

The collective transformation of the world requires the
continuous networking of an infinite array of otherwise impossible choices.

VII

Take care as you make the transition from bondage to freedom.
Even social relations worth fighting for are fragile.

DESTRUCTIVE CREATION, OR,
THE COMMUNISM OF THE SENSES
Alberto Toscano

'All who love their art seek the essence of technique to
show that which the eye does not see – to show truth,
the microscope and telescope of time, the negative of
time, the possibility of seeing without frontiers or dis-
tances; the tele-eye, sight in spontaneity, a kind of
Communist decoding of reality.' [1]

'How does one paint an ideology? … It does not suffice
simply to reproduce an image: an image charged with
ideology never makes itself see as the image of ideology.
It must be worked over in order to produce this minus-
cule interior distance, which unbalances it, identifies it,
and condemns it.' [2]

The divisions and variations internal to the very concept
of communism, in particular to its Marxian formulations, can serve as a privileged
point of entry into the political vicissitudes of contemporary art and current critical
interrogations regarding the entanglement of politics and aesthetics. Vice versa,
some light may be shed on the communist hypothesis in politics by the manner in
which it has been articulated, problematised and represented in the arts. In order to
evaluate the contemporary meaning of communism in and for art, one would need
to navigate through the four more or less doctrinal definitions of communism: as
the emancipation of human (and inhuman) *sensation*; as *ideology* (or proletarian
worldview); as a practice of *destruction* (of the status quo); and as a new type of *social
relation*. It is in the forcefield of tensions and contradictions, historical and theoretical,
generated by these four definitions that we may begin to glimpse how communism
could be artistically (and politically) reactivated or, to use a Deleuzian term, counter-
effectuated.

Though attention inevitably and immediately gravitates
towards the travails of the avant-gardes as companions, promoters or victims of the
communist enterprise in its Soviet guise – to propagandists and fellow travellers, to the
militant and the ostracised – communism and the aesthetic have been clinched tight
from day one. In the more anthropological amongst Marx's own writings, the aesthetic
problem of communism is exquisitely one of man's capacity both to produce and to
sense, as this capacity is variously stifled, transformed and *alienated* in the divided
conditions of labour under the domination of capital. Tellingly, and problematically,
when the communist future isn't subject in a proto-Taylorist geometry of discipline (as
in Engels's *On Authority*), the few 'images' of a liberated communist humanity provided
by (the early) Marx and Engels – scornful as they nevertheless were of those writing
'recipes for the cookshops of the future' – are bound to an aesthetic utopia. As Marx
wrote in *The German Ideology*,

'The exclusive concentration of artistic talent in particular individuals, and its suppression in the broad mass
which is bound up with this, is a consequence of divi-

sion of labour. Even if in certain social conditions, every one were an excellent painter, that would by no means exclude the possibility of each of them being also an original painter, so that here too the difference between 'human' and 'unique' labour amounts to sheer nonsense. In any case, with a communist organisation of society. there disappears the subordination of the artist to local and national narrowness, which arises entirely from division of labour, and also the subordination of the individual to some definite art, making him exclusively a painter, sculptor, etc.; the very name amply expresses the narrowness of his professional development and his dependence on division of labour. In a communist society there are no painters but only people who engage in painting among other activities. [3]

The 'communist organisation of society' is thus to be understood, aesthetically, as a domain of generalised (or generic) *singularity*, in which there is no contradiction (indeed no difference), between the *human* and the *unique*. This regime of singularity is explicitly formulated in terms of universalisation (the detachment from any 'local and national' narrowness, as well as from any geographically specialised role within the world market) and of the obliteration of genre, as well as of professional distinction. Generic communist humanity is here a humanity without genre, and communist organisation is a mechanism for the elimination of distinction, as a sociological indicator of power and hierarchy. To get to the root of the matter, the *expropriation* of capitalism – the obliteration of the division of labour and of its foundations in exploitation and property – is the opportunity for the reappropriation of man. As Marx has it in his Paris manuscripts of 1844: 'Communism is the *positive* supersession of *private property* as *human self-estrangement*, and hence the true *appropriation* of the *human* essence through and for man'. [4] Leaving the term 'aesthetic' to oscillate between its doctrinal, historical, philosophical and 'physiological' (*aesthesis* = sensation) acceptations, we might want to ask what is the aesthetic dimension in and of this essence? What does Marx intend when he speaks in the same notebooks of communism as a 'fully developed naturalism' which 'equals humanism'? What 'metabolic' function might art be accorded if communism is to be grasped as 'the realized naturalism of man and the realized humanism of nature'? And can we still operate with a humanist communism of sensations in the light of the machinic communism that is so forcefully proposed in Lenin's famous slogan about electricity and Soviets, which was in turn so inventively and subversively instantiated in Dziga Vertov's cinematic (and kinematical) practice? To disentangle some of these questions it is worth delving a little more into Marx's often ignored 'aesthetic' thinking – his own political logic of sensation.

The very domain whose 'real abstractions' Marx will employ his later years in hunting down and dissecting the economy, is itself defined in 'aesthetic' terms. Before developing his social dialectic of the commodity form in the theory of *fetishism* (which has its own 'aesthetic' references, the 'original' fetish being a ritual artefact, and commodities themselves being displayed in an intricate play of veiling and unveiling) Marx will approach the realm of the economic on the basis of that kind of sensual materialism he had learned from Feuerbach: 'This *material*, immediately *sensuous* private property is the material, sensuous expression of *estranged*

human life'. Economic alienation is thus both an *anaesthesia* of man's most intimate creative (or better, objectifying) capacities *and* something which is *felt*, in an almost tactile manner. The economy does not merely have a formal structure of appearance (as Marx will later painstakingly 'reveal'), it has an (alienating) material expression. Private property is 'sensuous'. The distribution of the sensible, to speak with Rancière, is here extremely complex, since the sense is *both* on the side of estranged human life and of the estranging economy. Or, capitalist distribution (as founded on the exploitation of that productive commodity, man) is for Marx the key abstract machine in the distribution of the sensible, in the expropriation of man's senses, now in the service of his own estrangement, and of the absorption of sensuousness by property itself: 'In *everyday, material industry…* we find ourselves confronted with the *objectified powers of the human essence*, in the form of *sensuous, alien, useful objects*, in the form of estrangement'.
[5] Both at the level of labour (power) and that of the product (the sensuous commodity, the object of estrangement) what is called for in the early Marx is a psychology of industry which is at one and the same time an aesthetics of the economy.

As many have noted, Marx's ontology is indeed a relational one, and the sensuousness that the economy leeches off the worker is paralleled by a transfer of relationality from humans to things (or, more precisely, commodities other than labour power).[6] Far from merely pitting humans against things – in what would inevitably be a losing, or rather a self-defeating, battle – Marx recognises the necessity of objects, as indispensable materialisations of human activity. The 'object, which is the direct activity of his individuality, is at the time his existence for other men, their existence and their existence for him'.[7] Anachronistically speaking, the object is a sort of 'interface' between man's individual creativity and his collective sociality. Sensuousness – whether creative or estranged – is always a shared, partitioned sensuousness. Productively and aesthetically, man is a 'social individual'. But an object – the concretion of human effort and ingenuity – is not (necessarily) a commodity, and the 'aesthetic' (and revolutionary) question thus concerns the possibility of a use of objects which would not be subordinated to the impersonal and inhuman sensorium of capitalism itself.

Private property, like the capitalism of which it is an intimate component, is of course not a simple evil for Marx, to be banished unthinkingly. Far from it, it is through private property – with its bloody and barbarous history – that man can treat himself (which is to say his relations) as an object, and thus be transformed: 'Private property is the sensuous expression of the fact that man becomes objective for himself.' So what kind of objectivity and sensuality is heralded by communism? First and foremost, appropriation should not be seen as a kind of humanist and metaphysical hypostasis of property: 'the positive supersession of private property, i.e. the *sensuous* appropriation of the human essence and human life, of objective man and of human *works* by and for man, should not be understood only in the sense of *direct*, one-sided *consumption*, of *possession*, of *having*'. Rather, the organised onset of communism is to be understood as a radical upheaval in the very structure of relationality, and, in a 'naturalistic' vein, this transformation is to be physiological, organic.

> 'All his *human* relations to the world – seeing, hearing, smelling, tasting, feeling, thinking, contemplating, sensing, wanting, acting, loving – in short all the organ of his individuality, like the organs which are directly communal in form, are in their *objective* approach or in their *approach to the object* the appropriation of that

object. This appropriation of *human* reality, their
aproach to the object, is the *confirmation of human rea
ity*. It is human *effectiveness* and human *suffering*, for
suffering, humanly conceived, is an enjoyment of the self
for man.'

No longer mediated by the sensuousness of property,
man is capable of developing 'directly communal' organs, with this community being
understood in terms of certain relation to the *object*. In the *'life of private property'*
on the contrary, the social character of individuality cannot be experienced, and man
remains estranged, alienated from the community of sensation. Note how, contrary
to those anaesthetic utopias whereby emancipated man would drift along in somatic
bliss, Marx has a profound anthropological sense for the complex nature of sensation,
whose logic implies than man may take 'enjoyment' not only in 'effectiveness', but also
in *suffering*. Communism is also, for Marx, the social appropriation of pain, no longer
stifled by the sovereignty of the 'sense of having'.[8]
    To be *sensuous* – i.e. to be real – is to be an object of
sense, a *sensuous* object, and thus to have sensuous objects outside oneself, objects
of one's sense-perception. To be sensuous is to *suffer* (to be subjected to the actions of
another. Man as an object of sensuous being is therefore a *suffering* being, and because
he feels his suffering (Leiden), he is a passionate (leidenschaftliches) being. Passion is
man's essential power vigorously striving to attain its object.[9]
    Marx's aesthetics of pain has nothing decadent or
morbid about it, precisely because the experience of suffering is not to be imagined as
a lonely pursuit, a mark of refinement and distinction, but as a corollary of a social (or
transindividual) mode of perceiving.[10] One cannot emphasise enough the uniqueness
of Marx's concept of a social organ (and social organisation) of perception, whereby,
within communism, sociality is an intimate aspect of the individual: 'the senses and
enjoyment of other men have become my *own* appropriation. Apart from these direct
organs, *social* organs are therefore created in the *form* of society; for example, activity
in direct association with others, etc., has become an organ of my *life expression* and
a mode of appropriation of *human* life.' And further: 'immediate *sensuous nature* for
man is, immediately, human sense perception (an identical expression) in the form of
the *other* man who is present in his sensuous immediacy for him'.[11]
    From a critical standpoint, however, we could say that
Marx here belongs to the 'subjectivist' history of aesthetics, from Homer to Nietzsche,
laid out by Heidegger in the first volume of his *Nietzsche*, to the extent that for Marx
'my object can only be the confirmation of one of my essential powers'. His social
aesthetics can be read in terms of an expression, externalisation or self-objectification
of an *essential human* capacity, whose sociality sometimes appears more innate than
constructed. And yet, the structure of Marx's inexorably *political* project is that it is
only with the 'communist organisation of society', which is to say, only after a thorough
revolution and destruction of the status quo, that what was in a sense always already
there, the transcendentally social structure of human sensing, can emerge and unfold.
Only in an organised and voluntary act can human 'essence' (*qua* ensemble of social
relations) structure society – this is, after all, the temporal structure of emancipation.
This is also felt in the theorisation of the link between communism and nature. It is
through the existence of a *humanised* nature, and the specific objects of the senses that
all the senses including the '*human* sense, the humanity of the senses' can be brought
forth. And emancipation can only be concrete once it organises a means to liberate the

aesthetic from the domination of need, of the realm of necessity: '*Sense* which is a prisoner of crude practical need has only a *restricted* sense'. This 'restricted' sense remains an 'abstract' sense of 'abstract' objects (as 'food' is for a starving man).

Capitalism, as a system of exploitation built, if not on the bare life, at least on the abstract labour and concrete domination of workers, is also viewed by Marx as a kind of anaesthetic machine (it would be interesting to think of the forms of anaesthesia, some by way of hedonic hyper-stimulation, which have marked the history of capitalism). Taking as its standard – its '*universal* standard, in the sense that it applies to the mass of men – the *worst possible state of privation* which life (existence) can know', the capitalist 'turns the worker into a being with neither needs nor senses and turns the worker's activity into a pure abstraction from all activity', whence the ideal of 'the ascetic but productive slave'. [12] The less you are, the more we have… Anticipating the grim aperçus of Horkheimer and Adorno, Marx thus writes of life under capitalism that 'its true manner of enjoyment is therefore *self-stupefaction*, this *apparent* satisfaction of need, this civilisation *within* the crude barbarism of need'. [13]

Communism, as the politics of human emancipation, and as the 'real movement which abolishes the present state of things, cannot therefore but be a radically sensory question: 'The supersession of private property is therefore the complete *emancipation* of all human sense and attributes'. But what has happened to the concept of emancipation as it has passed through the filters of anti-humanism, whether artistic or philosophical? What is an emancipation that would instead take a formal, subtractive or machinic guise? In the end, is emancipation irreducibly 'aesthetic'?

In the twentieth century, the sombre realities of political action have often obliged one to answer 'no' to that last question. And yet some thinkers have tried to cleave as closely as possible to the research programme laid out by Marx in those early writings. Chief amongst them is probably Herbert Marcuse. Much, if not all, of Marcuse's work rests on these pages of Marx on the emancipation of the senses. Indeed, it lies behind the position advocated in his last work *The Aesthetic Dimension*. There, Marcuse writes,

> 'Unlike orthodox Marxist aesthetics, I see the political potential of art in art itself, in the aesthetic form as such. Furthermore, I maintain that due to its aesthetic form, art is amply autonomous *vis-à-vis* the given social relations. In its autonomy, art both denounces these relations and at the same time transcends them. In this way, art subverts the dominant consciousness, common experience.'

The link to the 1844 Manuscripts is worth stressing because, unlike Adorno, Marcuse's conviction regarding the emancipatory impetus or political potential of art is not based simply on it being a vehicle of negativity and an exposition of the administered world – it is also the immediately sensuous dimension, indeed the *biological* dimension of artistic experience which preoccupies Marcuse (thus returning us to Marx's singular discussion of social organs of perception). Having said that, the themes of autonomy and transcendence indicate a crucial element that Marcuse shares with a 'classical' tradition in Marxist aesthetics, which sought to be both didactic and critical. This is the idea that art works as a force of anti-ideological disruption by its articulation not just of negativity, but also of a kind of *distance*, a *gap vis-à-vis* the status quo. [14] How such an aesthetics of distance, which is also an aesthetics of dissent, is rendered compatible with a kind of 'naturalism' regarding sensation is one of the interesting questions raised by a reading of Marcuse – and indeed by trying to articulate Marx's early politics of sensation with his mature critique of political economy. A further, perhaps incidental point, is that to some extent Marcuse's late position intersects the one broached in some of Jacques Rancière's recent writings. For instance, when Marcuse writes that, aside from its immanent aesthetico-political dimension, 'art's relation to praxis is inexorably indirect, mediated and vanishing' – something which could certainly be said, from Rancière's perspective, for the democracy of the aesthetic regime in the writings of Flaubert, as contrasted with the democratic disruption effectuated by an organised political subject, a subject of dissensus.

In his investigation of the aesthetic dimension then, Marcuse wishes to remain with the centrality of the emancipation of the senses, as an antidote to *the reification of Marxist theory itself*. The antidote is not just provided by an attention to the senses but also by the theme of aesthetic *transcendence*. How do these two dimensions, seemingly prohibited by the original Marxian framework, come together? Marcuse's answer involves the dialectic of sublimation and desublimation within aesthetic form,

> 'In the name of aesthetic form, given reality is necessarily *sublimated*: the immediate content is stylised, the 'data' are remodelled and reordered in accordance with the demands of aesthetic form, according to which even the representation of death and destruction evoke the need of hope, a need rooted in the new consciousness incorporated into the artwork. Aesthetic sublimation promotes the affirmative, conciliating component of art, even though it is at the same time the vehicle of the critical, negating function of art. The transcendence of immediate reality shatters the reified objectivity of constituted social relations and opens a new dimension of experience: the rebirth of rebel subjectivity. So, on the basis of aesthetic sublimation, we obtain a desublimation in the perception of individuals, their feelings, judgements, thoughts; an invalidation of dominant norms, needs and values. With all of its characteristics of ideology and confirmation, art remains a force of dissensus.'

Therefore this 'dis-sensus' is, in Marcuse's stance, simultaneously a matter of desublimating the senses and of sublimating form. And yet, even if we maintain an inextricable link between the being of communism and the being of sensation, even if we go to the extent of positing something like a communism of sensations – must this remain within the bounds of *human* sensation, within the parameters of emancipation set out by Marx in 1844?

We can turn here to that moment in Soviet cinema – perhaps the consummate emblem of communist art – when an aesthetically revolutionary cell, around the director Dziga Vertov, sought to mutate the eye from theatrical spectator to a revolutionary 'agent of critical production'.[15] Born of an explosive merger of political aesthetics and aesthetic politics, the documents issued by Vertov's Council of Three (in which he was flanked by Mikhail Kaufman, his brother, the eponymous 'man with a move camera', and Elizaveta Svilova, his wife and editor) identify a *subject* (the *kinoks* or 'cinema-eye men'), an *enemy* ('Cinematography' as theatre of memory and representation of man: '"Cinematography" must die so that the art of cinema may live. WE *call for its death to be hastened*'), a name for *being* (movement), and the basic *element* of aesthetic construction and articulation (the interval). Moreover, however restricted and familial Vertov's cell, they indicate one of the key aspects of the avant-garde's response to the problem of communism and art: the need to anticipate communist social relations (of production, distribution, and consumption – as well as collaboration) within art-making itself, to make the fashioning of new *aesthetic* relations simultaneously into the eliciting of new *social and political* relations.

Throughout the texts produced by this group we can identify three crucial demands, related respectively to the question of genre, the struggle with the aesthetic of humanism and the relation to politics: (1) 'The cinema must die so that the art of cinema may live. (2) 'The eye must be emancipated from man.' (3) 'We still need a cinematic October.' The first demand is strikingly encapsulated in a poem contained within an 'appeal' from 1922. Confrontationally adopting the second person, addressed amongst others to 'You – exhausted by memories', this text seeks to dramatise the death of a cinema of representations (or even of Eisensteinian 'attractions', still too 'thematic' for the *kinoks*) as the necessary prelude to the emergence of a cinema that would develop the autonomous life of sensation in the montage of movement. The sheer violence of the image is striking, a violence done directly to the cinema as *organism*.

'A friendly warning: / Don't hide your heads like ostriches. / Raise your eyes. / Look around you – / There! / It's obvious to me / as to any child / The innards, / the guts of strong sensations / are tumbling out / of cinema's belly, / ripped open on the reef of revolution. / See them dragging along, / leaving a bloody trail on the earth / that quivers with horror and disgust. / It's all over.'

Are we still in the ambit of the Marxian problematic of social organs? Sensation (or movement), revealed by the incision of the Vertovian image of cinema, bears an arresting affinity with Adorno's demand *à propos* of the New Music from Darmstadt: 'it would be necessary to eliminate unsentimentally every vestige of the organic that does not originate in its principle of artifice, its thoroughgoing organisation'.[16] Vertov does not oppose the *mechanism* of montage to the *organic body* of cinema. He dissolves this opposition in order to demonstrate how the new cinema transfigures the physiological and theatrical eye of the habituated spectator into a kino-eye, a sort of transhuman conduit for a life of sensation that can only be experienced in its vital truth to the degree that it is machinically constructed and composed. In other words, the emancipation of the senses demands an emancipation (of the camera-eye) *from* the senses, and, in a sense, an emancipation from the human. Here the relationship between technological and aesthetic innovation, on the one hand, and the political logic of sensation, on the other, means that the communist imperative to abolish, to destroy the present state of things turns into an attempt to abolish (or at least radically transform) the very organs of social perception. Without an anthropology of sensation – except for a condemning and anti-humanist one – Vertov's art, in its deep polemical urge, often hovers around the point of convergence between communist emancipation and nihilist obliteration.

In this respect it is congruent with one of the key traits discerned by T.J. Clark in the War Modernism, so to speak, of Malevich and his colleagues, which he explains as follows: 'It is because War Communism was both chaos and rationality, both apocalypse and utopia – because it presented itself as such, in a flurry of apocalypse and utopia – that it gave rise to the modernism we are looking at.'[17] Clark writes of 'the extraordinary being-together in 1920 of the grossest struggle with the realm of necessity and the grandest (or at least, most overweening) attempt to imagine necessity otherwise. Imagining otherwise was for a while actually instituted as part of the state apparatus'.[18] In his remarkable study on Stalinism as *Gesamtkunstwerk*, Boris Groys will go even farther arguing that, far from the Soviet avant-garde being simply betrayed by the socialist realist reaction and the nationalist productivism that followed the second revolution of 1929, 'the Stalinist epoch realised the fundamental demand of the avant-garde, the passage from the art of the representation of life to its transfiguration in the framework of a total aesthetico-political project'.[19] The UNINOVIS (an acronym for 'Affirmers of New Forms in Art') group to which Malevich belonged, along with Lissitsky, had indeed anticipated the all-powerful plan as a political and aesthetic object, positing the Economy as in a sense the subject and object of art (Marx's critiques having been forgotten or crushed underfoot by the productivist drive). Interestingly, this hypostasis of the Economy went hand in hand not with a social individual as discussed in Marx's manuscripts (texts which incidentally went undiscovered until 1932), but with a kind of aesthetic and mystical fusion of individual and collective, an artistic image of communist nihilism: 'if we want to attain perfection, the self must be annihilated – just as religious fanatics annihilate themselves in the face of the divine, so the modern saint must annihilate himself in the face of the "collective", in the face of that "image" which perfects itself in the name of unity, in the name of coming-together'.[20]

This dovetails with the second demand contained in the declarations of Vertov's Council of Three. The 'emancipation of the camera' from the habituated eye is the very condition for the 'inhuman' experience of the life of sensation. Together with many of his contemporaries, Vertov will thus come, in this cinema which could be termed a 'communism of sensations' or a 'communism of movements', to equate the promise of revolution with a liberation from the human depicted as a *habitus* of representation. In Vertov's cinema the revolution is in principle the harbinger of an unfettered, inhuman sensation. In the transvaluation of the eye into the 'kino-eye', we glimpse the promise – at the intersection of political and aesthetic militancy – that the emancipation of human subjects will entail the emancipation of the inhuman from the representational *habitus* of humanity. Yes, this is a break from reality into the real but into a real that will never be sundered from its construction.

> 'The mechanical eye, the camera, rejecting the human eye as crib sheet, gropes its way through the chaos of visual events, letting itself be drawn or repelled by movement, probing, as it goes, the path of its own movement. It experiments, distending time, dissecting movement, or, in contrary fashion, absorbing time within itself, swallowing years, thus schematising processes of long duration inaccessible to the normal eye.'

Vertov's cinema is thus marked by a systematic *anachronism*, a capacity to 'denature' time and envelop it, along with movement, as an element, material, or rather, as a *medium* of construction. But both the time and character of Vertov's cinematic emancipation in a way invert Marx, for whom the emancipation of the senses was inseparable from a thoroughgoing socialisation and humanisation.

'The eye has become a *human* eye, just as its object has become a social, *human* object, made by man for man. The *senses* have therefore become *theoreticians* in their immediate praxis. They relate to the thing for its own sake, but the thing itself is an *objective human relation* to itself and to man, and vice-versa. Need or enjoyment have therefore lost their egoistic nature, and nature has lost its mere *utility* in the sense that its use has become *human* use.' [21]

Vertov's own project of anti-humanist emancipation will instead come up against the humanist inhumanity of Stalinism, wrecked by the hardening of the revolution, by a socialist state which could endure only insofar as it was itself endlessly and expediently *represented*, albeit at times through the formidable talents of the surviving constructivists (see, for instance, the remarkable propaganda publication, for foreign use, 'USSR in Construction', in which Lissitsky himself took part). Whether or not we concur with Clark's diagnosis of the 'horrors of modernity', the political and aesthetic catastrophe suffered by the likes of Vertov was indeed horrific. In the notes and journals that track the disintegration of the *kinoks* and Vertov's increasing desperation at his marginality we can read the following, grimly physical description from 1934,

'We went about covered from head to foot with naphtaline, our irritated skins unable to breathe, smeared with stinking caustic liquids, fighting off attacks of lice. Our nerves were always on edge, and we controlled them by willpower. We did not want to give up. We had decided to fight to the finish.'

The third demand, that of an 'October in cinema', does not go away. What does this demand entail? *That the art of the revolution must never represent the revolution.* A generalised parallelism must be invented between political and artistic militancy, the services rendered by the latter taking the form of an *enactment* of the revolution, a *transposition* of revolutionary injunctions into its own domain, specified to its own categories (not the people, but movement; not the party member, but the *kinok*; not labour, but the interval...)

In the end, Vertov's tragically enthusiastic machinic communism may be linked to the aesthetic dimension promoted by Marcuse, when the latter writes that the 'truth of art consists in its capacity to shatter the monopoly of constituted reality (that is of those who constituted it) and to *define* what is *real*. In this break, which is the conquest of the aesthetic form, the fictitious world of art appears as the true reality'. But, as the most faithful and inventive epigones of Vertov knew (especially Chris Marker and his comrades in the collective and worker-led cinema groups, like the *Groupes Medvedkine* and the production unit SLON) [22] the destructive creation of new forms and the shattering of the 'monopoly of constituted reality' (or, as the filmmaker Peter Watkins would have it, the MONOFORM) is inseparable from the generation of new, communist social relations. [23] This requirement cannot be satisfied by 'the re-presentation as aesthetics of what was once social interaction, political discourse, and even ordinary human relations'. [24] And that is indeed because, following the political aesthetics immanent to Marx's notion of emancipation, the production of new sensory relations is inextricable from the real movement of abolishing the old ones.

NOTES.
1. Dziga Vertov, quoted in the Annette Michelson's introduction to *Kino-Eye: The Writings of Dziga Vertov*, University of California Press, Berkeley and Los Angeles,1984.

2. Louis Althusser, 'Sur Lucio Fanti', in *Écrits philosophiques et politiques, tome II*, STOCK/IMEC, Paris, 1997, pp. 612-63.

3. Karl Marx (with Friedrich Engels), *The German Ideology*, Prometheus Books, Amherst, 1998, pp. 417-48.

4. Karl Marx, *Early Writings*, trans. R. Livingstone and G. Benton, Penguin, London, 1975, p. 348.

5. Ibid. p. 354.

6. See, for instance, Étienne Balibar, *The Philosophy of Marx*, Verso, London, 1995, pp. 32-3.

7. *Early Writings* p. 349.

8. Ibid. p. 352.

9. Ibid. p. 390.

10. *The Philosophy of Marx*, p.30.

11. *Early Writings*, p. 355.

12. Ibid. p. 360.

13. Ibid. p. 363.

14. This position is given a potent anti-humanist inflection in Louis Althusser's writings on art. Writing of Brecht, Althusser sees the brilliance of his theatre and its alienation effect in being able to inscribe the distance between staged representation and reality within the stage itself. Equally, meditating on the painters Cremonini and Fanti, Althusser presses with this theme of the exposure of gaps and the production of displacements as key to the anti-ideological function of art. In particular, in Cremonini

Althusser glimpses the possibility of moving from ideological 'abstract painting' to the anti-ideological function of 'painting the abstract', which is to say, the capacity to paint, or to expose, relationality itself. For Althusser, Cremonini is able to inscribe into his own paintings his own 'abstract relations' to the painting within the painting itself, turning these relations into its very 'matter'. He does not paint faces (the faces, inevitably, of subjects of interpellation), or deformity, but processes of deformation. Thus, both in its form and in its content this art moves against the ideology of the creator and the consumer, the ideology of full, social and aesthetic relationality under capitalism. Real works of art let us 'perceive' (and not know) in some sense from within, by an interior distance, the very ideology in which they are caught. The freedom of man passes through the knowledge of real, abstract relations – this is why, in aesthetics as well as politics, Althusser can hold that theoretical anti-humanism is the necessary prelude to practical humanism. See the section 'Écrits sur l'art' in *Écrits philosophiques et politiques, tome II*, pp. 553-620.

15. Annete Michelson in *The Writings of Dziga Vertov*, p. xix. All quotes from *Vertov and the Council of Three* are from this collection.

16. Theodor W. Adorno, 'Vers une musique informelle', in *Quasi una Fantasia: Essays on Modern Music*, Verso, London,1998.

17. T.J. Clark, *Farewell to an Idea: Episodes in a History of Modernism*, Yale University Press, New Haven, 2001, p. 242.

18. ibid. p. 245.

19. Quoted from the Italian translation of Groys's *Gesamtkunstwek Stalin. Die gespaltene Kultur in der*

Soujetunion: Lo stalinismo ovvero l'opera d'arte totale, Garzanti, Milan, 1992, p. 48.

20. Kasimir Malevich, *UNOVIS Almanac I*, June 1920, quoted in *Farewell to an Idea*, p. 226.

21. *Early Writings*, p. 352.

22. See Catherine Lupton, *Chris Marker: Memories of the Future*, Reaktion, London, especially Chapter 5, 'A Grin without a Cat', on the period of Marker's militant collaborations between 1967 and 1977. For a detailed account of the new social, productive and distributive relations established in this cinematic practice, through the prism of one of Marker's collective projects, see Laurent Véray, *Loin du Vietnam*, Paris, 2004. The militant films jointly done by Marker, his comrades, and factory workers from Besançon and Sochaux are now collected in 2 DVDs published by Editions Montparnasse, *Les Groupes Medvedkine*, 2006.

23. Peter Watkins, *The Media Crisis*, available at: http://www.mnsi.net/~pwatkins/PW_Statement.htm.

24. Julian Stallabrass, writing *à propos* of 'relational aesthetics' in *Art Incorporated*, Oxford University Press, Oxford, 2004, p. 182. Nicolas Bourriaud does indeed speak of a 'formal communism' in his book *Postproduction* to identify the new artistic tendency to the production of novel 'modes of sociality' and the development of seemingly non-commoditised forms of cultural reappropriation. Without sounding too maximalist, we could say that without the real and creative movement of abolishing (rather than escaping) the present state of things, communism will precisely only ever remain... formal. In other words, I suspect that the 'communism of forms' is perfectly compatible with the communism... of capital.

THE
COUNCIL
OF THE
BEES

OR,

Something About Communism Maybe.

CONTAINING MANY RARE
OBSERVATIONS OF BEES AND ALLEGORICAL
MATERIALS OF THE HIGHEST QUALITY.

BELFAST :
Printed for *Factotum* of Donegall Street, MMVI

Multiple reflections of a little girl in the
facets of a bee's compound eye.

THE PREFACE

A worker lands among his friends
Who set their tools aside and lend
Their ears to learn what he has thought
And seen; for contemplation's taught
Him politics, the heavens and philosophy,
That's marked him from the other bees.

The smallest point beneath the sky,
This grumbling and debating hive;
When led beyond their daily strife
To estimate the span of life,
To weigh the value of their labour,
Of Justice, power, of nectar's savour;
Can entertain a grub's deserts
Or calculate the universe.

It's said of bee society,
Not ruled by Wild Democracy,
That millions endeavour to supply
Each other's lust and vanity;*
Or that laws of Nature do pertain
And Anarchy without confusion reigns,†
But this is eighteenth-century politicks
When poets were not naturalists.

A drone can understand the world
Coloured, of course, by what they're told.
Each worker comprehends their state
With a compound eye, which relates
The fragments of the life they see
to the place of bees in history.

*In which the author describes a
philosophical bee, the breadth of bee
philosophy, the limitations of some
former accounts of bee society and what
philosophy is for.*

* BERNARD DE MANDEVILLE, *The
Grumbling Hive: or, Knaves Turn'd
Honest*, London, 1705

† ALEXANDER POPE, *Essay on Man*,
London, 1733

JANICE: All right Terry we're listening.

TERRY: I think this is an instructive tale; the story of a **WEIGHTLIFTER**.

Three bees discuss their lives by exchanging and discussing stories.

Tommy worked on the docks.
He was a forceful man,
Respected by all his fellow workers
For his brute strength.
One could find no better
for demanding physical rigours.

But Tommy only looked after number one.
He had no interest in the unions
And just worked to get paid.
He spent his money on himself
And didn't care about corruption
or his comrades being betrayed.

One day a strike came.
The workers united for better pay.
Tommy was having none of it;
He preferred to do things his own way.
He kept on working,
Through the pickets and the taunts.

In the evening he lifted weights.
Pumping iron was his distraction.
His thighs could crush onions.
Well into old age
He honed his body,
But his mind was a blank page

Then one day in his eightieth year,
Tommy went upstairs with his washing,
But he never made it to the top.
Halfway up his body had failed him,
Powerless like a child, he was alone,
With his weakness until he died.

Workers ejecting a Drone.

BASIL: So you're saying 'show solidarity with other
workers or you will die sad and alone'? It's a moral tale; the scab
gets his just deserts?

TERRY: What if the workers are wrong though?

JANICE: I think it's about the heaviness of corpses. I
have another story along the same lines, it's called
the **CROISSANT**.

In a small northern village called Comber,
That's known for its prodigious output of rolled material,
A young lad called Larkin was born.
It was a plain and righteous place.

The boy was a timid fellow and kept himself to himself,
He was a party member like his parents,
He had beans and sausages every day,
And in the morning Quaker Oats.

Nothing else tickled his fancy in a culinary way until
One day he came across a bakery and
Saw in the window a crescent shaped pastry
Dressed in the most tempting chocolate.

He imagined the taste of the croissant
but quickly banished the sensation from his mind
And raced home for his supper,
A limp helping of Welsh Rarebit and then to bed.

He drifted off to sleep,
But strange dreams awaited him.

Floating down main street past the bakery,
He saw a baker with a bee's head.

The baker said 'zzzzittt try my croissant,
It will make you see the light.
There's pleasure in exploring new sensations.
Zzzt go on take a bite.'

Young Larkin woke up in a cold sweat
And recalled what he had eaten in his dream.
His mind was filled with possibilities
Of a world of new tastes.

In the years that followed
Larkin consumed many
Fine and extravagant dishes.
Until one day a puffer fish came his way.

It contained some fatally poisonous liver fluid
Between the delicately flavoured flesh.
But Larkin ate it anyway and dropped dead,
on the spot, with his socks on.

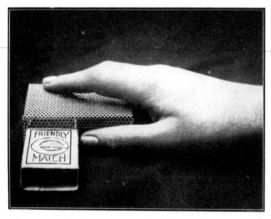

Transfering the Queen from Match-box to Cage.

BASIL: It's the same thing, self indulgence is rewarded with
death.

TERRY: No it's not, this is a counter-revolutionary parable,
he was only going to produce rolled materials until he started
stuffing his face. It is a kind of Epicurean Existentialism, what could
be more conservative?

JANICE: You don't like people enjoying themselves do you?

BASIL: When I heard your first story it reminded me of
the CHURCH OF THE EMPTY SIGNIFIER

Young Robin was an orphan
And lived in a hostel where
Her idiosyncratic behaviour was tolerated.
She was clearly an intelligent girl.

The night porter was the only person
She ever spoke to and to him she
Confided that she had a secret treasure:
A pair of Karl Marx's original underpants.

She had purchased them in a previous hostel
From an old man who had known Marx personally.
She referred to them as the 'Empty Signifier'.
Because they didn't mean that much without the man inside them.

The hostel had a garden shed which
Robin broke into secretly at night.
She started to transform it into
The *Church of the Empty Signifier*.

It had the pants and pictures,
From magazines mostly, around the walls.
There were heroes of the Revolution
And important members of the Party.

She left the hostel next Spring
And the gardener found the chapel,
When he came to cut the grass.
She had even left the pants behind.

JANICE: I like the bit about the underpants, do you think they really
were Marx's, there might be some trace of the man himself in a
trace-relic sort of way. The shed sounds like an installation.

TERRY: You're saying Communism is like a religion, you're saying
Marx was a smelly, you're saying 'it's all over'?
BASIL: I find my enjoyment tainted by regret, it makes me
think of the **ROUMANIAN SYNCHRONISED
SWIMMING TEAM IN THE 1980s**.

Burly women, like cranes, moving in perfect time,
Taught us all a lesson we will not soon forget.

Launched into the water, tight and together,
Industriously throwing balletic shapes.

A system that could harness such walrus power:
Just imagine their combine harvesters, we thought...

Collective action requires a hive-mind mentality.
Or so said Marika, the leader of the squad.

Those polar bear poetesses often spoke in aphorisms,
But that wasn't what daunted us.

Overcome were we, by their physical feat:
To swim the earth Eggbeater style in Float formation†.

The capitalists meanwhile were playing water polo,
as we were to find out; too late, sadly.

*An apiary guard whose all-day task is
the destruction of hornets.*

† FLOAT: A surface formation where
between two and eight swimmers are
connected horizontally.
EGGBEATER: A rotary action of the legs
used to support and propel the upper
body in an upright position, leaving the
arms free.

COLLAGES 1992–1995
CK Rajan

LIST OF PLATES
CK Rajan
All works collage on paper

Untitled
140 x 98 mm

Untitled
80 x 55 mm

Artles Fishing
155 x 200 mm

Portrait of Silence
135 x 190 mm

Ya Hi Hai Right Choice Aha!
175 x 130 mm

Untitled
120 x 165 mm

Untitled
125 x 165 mm

Untitled
105 x 180 mm

With special thanks to Anita Dube

FUTURE UNKNOWN
MACHIAVELLI FOR THE TWENTY-FIRST CENTURY
Gopal Balakrishnan

For a hundred years after 1848, defeats for the Left typically came in two, tightly intermeshed, forms. Crushing blows – 1849, 1871, 1919, 1926, 1939 – alternating with unexpected bouts of prosperity, could contain, for a time, the aspirations of those demanding more than the owners of society and their allies were prepared to concede. In the West, the great rebellions of the late 1960s broke with this pattern. The unprecedented affluence of the first postwar decades had shaped a generational milieu resistant to an older, middle-class work and leisure ethic, and receptive to insurgencies of the downtrodden. The subsequent sharp upswing in working-class militancy in the core, and setbacks for American imperialism on the periphery, briefly made it seem to some as if distant pre-revolutionary situations were looming in the homelands of capitalism.

In attenuated local forms, various legacies of these overlapping moments have survived the sweeping rounds of capitalist restructuring that followed the world's economic downturn of the mid-1970s. Despite this impressive feat of adaptation, such pockets of opposition have had difficulty coming to terms with the formidable staying power of a conservative/neoliberal ascendancy that is now in its third decade. In a parallel perhaps to the legendary failure of the interwar Left to comprehend the advances of fascism, opponents of this passive revolution have been unable to account for its great successes, as so far it seems to possess the historically unique ability to invent the standards by which it is judged. What accounts for the ease of its victories, often scored with sparing doses of coercion – 'democratically' – and yet in a context of declining fortunes for large majorities? The enervation of collective resistance under these conditions seems to signal the advent of an order of things in which praxis itself has become an enigma.

Times of open conflict between proponents of different social orders are, of course, historically exceptional. The keenest observers of nineteenth-century politics – Tocqueville, Heine, Donoso, Marx, Burkhardt, Nietzsche among them – underscored the novelty of a society in the throes of a chronic, publicly staged legitimation crisis. In 1929, Carl Schmitt captured the culmination of this historical experience in an epigram: 'We, in central Europe, live *sous l'oeil des Russes.*'[1] While organised counter-offensives played a significant role in the eventual neutralisation of this threat to the West, during the last decades of the twentieth century these specifically political thrusts were overtaken and subsumed by a broader structural transformation that has bypassed classical forms of both hegemony and resistance.

It is difficult to gauge the possibilities of effective intellectual intervention in such an opaque historical situation. The crux of the exchange between Stefan Collini and Francis Mulhern in these pages has been whether critical discourse needs to be anchored in deep political commitments in order to orient its targets, scope and polemical intensities.[2] The burden of Mulhern's case is that it is only in a political mode that society can be put into question, through sovereign affirmations and negations of its fundamental premises. One does not have to endorse Collini's notion of politics as a potentially open and endless conversation to recognise that both views seem to presume the existence of a largely superseded public sphere, where society once revealed its sensitivity to the pin pricks and salvos of critique. It could be that this contemporary closure of the political is merely a conjunctural, and thus reversible, effect of a quarter-century of sweeping victories for capital. Alternatively, we may be in the midst of a deeper transformation that has scrambled the very phenomenon of agency, relegating classical partisanships to the status of more or less eccentric, ideological preferences. Perhaps in a more ominous sense than he intended, this development confirms Collini's position.

        In the waiting chamber of the present, to what texts should we turn in determining a critical stance adequate to our situation? Thought experiments with previously inconceivable constitutions were the hallmark of classical political philosophy; it may be useful to revisit this genre, whose peaks had cast a shadow over every institution of human society in the long intervals before their actual negation seemed possible. From *The Republic* to *Emile*, this art of estrangement had the effect of making the most drastic transformations conceivable, if only in theory. Generally, however, even the most antinomian forms of this tradition have had little determinate relationship to political practice. The writings of Machiavelli form an exceptional case within this history, for instead of a critical, essentially idealistic, discourse on the absence of legitimacy, they offer a novel method for exploring the sheer potentiality of praxis: thinking through the inception, full scope and limits of the constituent power to construct new orders.

        In a posthumously published manuscript, Louis Althusser sought to convey the philosophical significance of Machiavelli's fragmentary thoughts on the traumatic origins of new states.[3] The point was not to offer a new interpretation of Machiavelli but rather, he reasoned, to recognise the impossibility of a definitive solution, as the creative statute of a new mode of political thought. The ellipses and antinomies of these texts were the nodal points of a buoyant ontology, enabling readers to imagine and to think the onset of action through a new literary form: the parable of innovation. I would like to propose that a more concrete thesis can be developed from this speculative point of departure, one that consists of two parts: Machiavelli's innovation was, firstly, to raise the distinctively modern problem of the actuality of the most radical projects of transformation; and secondly, to provide an attentive reader with a method of reflecting upon and generating effective practical stances with regard to continuing, renewing or abandoning such projects. This thesis can be tested by examining the decisive episodes in the centuries-long reception of Machiavelli's thought, and posing for our own times the question that earlier commentators considered to be the defining problem of the modern historical situation: what in the human condition can be changed through political praxis?

I

        An initial problem is whether classical political theory or philosophy can retain any relevance today, within the labyrinth of mediatic society.

        The charge that such works belong to an antiquarian genre cannot be dismissed out of hand. One influential reason offered for studying these canonical texts is that they provide an opportunity to reflect on alternative political orders, based upon different conceptions of human nature. If this were true, books of this kind should perhaps then be regarded as memorabilia for our post-political situation. While not many intellectuals like to assent to the finality of this verdict, most public discourse more or less enthusiastically accepts the absence of any alternatives to liberal democracy and free-market capitalism, with the main outstanding problem being the parameters of cultural tolerance. There are, of course, some volatile elements in this formula: a broad upswing of religious fundamentalism in the US; anti-immigrant backlashes in Europe. Elsewhere, numerous combinations of religion and ethnicity offer challenges but present no compelling alternatives to the governing norm.

This is the setting for the so-called crisis of 'the political' – a term whose very abstraction seems to signal an anxiety about the obsolescence of state-centred conceptions of politics and a related set of civic virtues. The study of classical political theory is often justified now in terms of an equally indeterminate call for a 'return of the political'. This takes the form of a number of conservative, liberal and radical variants on the multifarious tradition of 'civic republicanism', whose basic idea is that the virtues of active citizenship are needed to counteract the atomistic consequences of a modernity powered by the free play of interests and identities in civil society. Even those who are critical in some way of this mainstream democratese – admirers of Leo Strauss or, alternatively, Antonio Negri – acknowledge Machiavelli as the spiritual forefather of that Magna Carta of republican Empire, the US Constitution. Reinterpreting the Florentine should therefore have significant consequences for assessing the contemporary adequacy of this whole field of civic discourse.

The proposition that the political itself is on the wane might be confusing, as there has obviously been no decrease in politics *per se*. What is meant is an eclipse of 'high politics', of arms races between nations and classes in which the structure of society is at stake. The rhetoric of political exhaustion and closure dates from the restorations of the ninetheenth century. Alexis de Tocqueville.

> 'Will we never again [nota bene] see a fresh breeze of true political passions… of violent passions, hard though sometimes cruel, yet grand, disinterested, fruitful, those passions which are the soul of the only parties that I understand and to which I would gladly give my time, my fortune, and my life?' [4]

But one might ask: is such a radical repoliticisation even conceivable in the most advanced societies, or for that matter desirable? Behind the outpourings of nostalgia for more activist citizenries there lies a profound discomfort with the very idea of abandoning the security of the status quo – our deeply apolitical form of life. The claim that revolutionary praxis leads to totalitarian catastrophe enjoys the nearly universal assent of intellectual opinion. Attachment, openly acknowledged or not, to the status quo is at an historic high point.

II

Have Washington's international and domestic offensives of the last few years – with their still incalculable fallout – brought an end to this neutralised post-Cold War scene? For all the acrimony of the latest political season, the main control centres of responsible opinion still cleave to the neoliberal prescriptions of the past quarter-century. The flexibility of the system should never be underestimated yet, paradoxically, the absence of large-scale opposition has not prevented the main fixtures of the world political situation from entering into solution: the controversial shift from 'human rights' to 'anti-terrorism' as the ideological dominant of foreign policy; the unexpected sharpening of tensions between the US and core Europe; the military credibility of the American state put on the line for the first time in thirty years, as partisan war rages on the Tigris; growing strains on anti-proliferation accords; and, perhaps most significantly, looming economic turbulence stemming from the unsustainable American deficits that keep the whole world economy afloat. The current fiscal and financial environment, suggests a conservative historian of international bond markets, has all the makings of a perfect storm.[5]

In the era of neoliberalism, the great powers have dismantled much of their own regulatory capacity and unleashed the risk society, as if the harvests of market turbulence could be reaped forever. The reflux of this Great Transformation is putting into question some of the main trend-lines that seemed to be locked in place after the end of the Cold War. The optimistic narrative of globalisation – the dominant ideology of the last decade – is in retreat. Polanyi's account of the nineteenth-century era of world market capitalism as setting the stage for the hard landings of the inter-war era offers an instructive precedent. The only reason why a crisis of such proportions still seems improbable is that there are currently no powers of any consequence that could see their interests furthered by capitalising on this disorder.

III

This is the context for a return to Machiavelli, a figure that comes into full force within a historical situation whose outlines and possibilities cannot be grasped within the existing terms of political thought, as a result of the increasingly problematic reality – even irreality – of praxis. His own formative moment came with the abrupt collapse of the world of Italian city-states at the end of the fifteenth century, in the wake of invading foreign armies and domestic regime changes. In the midst of this flood, Machiavelli announces a break in time; or rather, the emergence of a new politically constituted temporality of epochs. The advent of discontinuity comes with a founding gesture of radical disjunction from the recent past – 'these corrupt centuries of ours'[6] – demarcated from a classical period, and a present that opens onto a dramatically widened horizon.[7]

The opening Preface of the *Discourses on Livy* could be said to have two introductory paragraphs. The first begins with a comparison of the dangers of finding new methods and systems to those faced by an explorer seeking 'unknown waters and lands'; and with a declaration of intent: 'I have decided to take a path as yet untrodden by anyone'.[8] The second begins with a blunt dismissal of Renaissance antiquarianism as poor imitation of the ancients, whose greatness did not reside in carving statues but rather in the sovereign art of making history. This Janus-faced beginning underscores the perspectival problems of the narrative categories with which we attempt to grasp the structure of historical situations. In the preface to the second book of *Discourses*, while Machiavelli concedes that it is impossible to know history *wie es eigentlich gewesen war* from the disparate, tendential accounts of victors and survivors, there is nevertheless a method of interrogating the reasoning of these accounts, of seeing how conditions have varied from 'province to province'.[9]

There is no shortage of social theories that purport to explain large-scale historical crises and transformations, and which address more directly the dynamics of the contemporary world-system. What can one learn from reading Machiavelli's texts today that could not be found in the writings of Marx, for example? The latter, it is often said, did not adequately account for specifically political categories, forms and praxes. The previously missing dimension of citizenship, nationality, party and so on, introduced to supplement – or, alternatively, supersede – Marx, is invariably ideological, in the Althusserian sense of a language of subjective orientation. Reading Machiavelli in this context offers us the prospect of a philosophical interrogation of the ideologies of agency that inform these political – actor-oriented – conceptions of history.

Machiavelli's writings are a sustained investigation into the limits of political enterprise without the closure of any anthropological essentialism. It is true that he often seems interested in the foundation of new political orders – religions, states, peoples – as a way of framing the anterior problem of the plasticity of 'human nature'. But the disparate reflections he offers on the latter do not form the basis of either conservative prudence or utopian desire, but rather act to constantly unsettle both. The 'badness' Machiavelli refers to is political rather than moral, still less theological: it does not stem 'from the wicked nature of men, as they used to say'.[10] Further, this badness, it turns out, is not all bad, politically speaking.

> 'Men are desirous of new things, so much so that most often those who are well off desire newness as much as those who are badly off. For as was said before, and it is true, men get bored with the good and grieve in the ill.'[11]

To radicalise the problem of founding a state reveals the possibility of a new art of founding peoples, raising armies and winning battles. This in turn brings into view the radical, inhuman virtues of those who aim to reinvent human beings.[12] The movement of Machiavelli's thought is startling. First he tells us: 'I do not know whether this has ever occurred or whether it is possible'. Then, that it would be a 'very cruel enterprise or altogether impossible'. Next, how it could be done:

> 'To make in cities new governments with new names, new authorities, new men; to make the rich poor, the poor rich… to build new cities, to take down those built, to exchange the inhabitants from one place to another; and in sum, not to leave anything untouched.'[13]

As Rousseau, one of Machiavelli's most astute readers, put it: 'He who dares to undertake the establishment of a people should feel that he is, so to speak, in a position to change human nature'.[14] In a work ostensibly devoted to the study of republics, the provisional legitimation of such methods explosively broadens the scope of what is thinkable beyond the limits set by the prevailing conventions of civic discourse. Could such a figure of absolute radical agency come into existence today? The answer must take into account an immense variability in the potency and knowledge of men in different times and places: 'the weakness of men at present, caused by their weak education and their slight knowledge of things, makes them judge ancient judgements in part inhuman, in part impossible.'[15]

Machiavelli's thoughts on this subject are far from conclusive; he seems to contradict himself interminably when it comes to this very point of how transformable human beings are, how open to change. Before he even begins his account of the lives of the makers and would-be makers of new states, he warns those who would take up arms against their masters, believing they could fare better, that 'they are deceived because they see later by experience that they have done worse.'[16] One could provide a long list of observations and maxims from *The Prince* and the *Discourses on Livy* that negate each other, leaving the reader looking for a solution. The most disconcerting of these concerns the epistemological legitimacy of strategic reasoning in terms of historical precedents and counterfactuals. While Machiavelli seems to scorn those who judge that 'imitation is not only difficult but impossible – as if heavens, sun, elements, men had varied in their motion, order and power from what they were in antiquity', he later goes on to write: 'because like causes happen rarely, it will also occur rarely that like remedies avail'.[17]

What is the significance of these seeming aporias? As Althusser noted: 'the central point where everything is tied up endlessly escapes detection'.[18] In classical political philosophy, such signals of doubt arguably convey a teaching about the wisdom of moderation. This is not what happens in Machiavelli. The stories he tells prompt the reader to reflect on how to discern, how practically to orient oneself towards potential courses of action in exemplary situations. Here aporias raise questions that do not paralyse, or moderate, but move the reader to recognise the advantages – often tenuously demonstrated – of the impetuous course. Machiavelli concedes that this kind of strategic lore is a very precarious kind of knowing; nevertheless he persistently encourages the most immoderate stances. In the fundamental strategic binary he establishes between 'temporise' or 'strike', the line of reasoning always tilts towards the latter.[19]

There is perhaps a theoretical justification for this rhetoric of going to the extreme, since such courses of action seem to provide the best food for his manner of thought. The scenarios Machiavelli depicts in his ancient and contemporary parables are constructed to test the mettle of various perspectives and stances towards the world: personalised *Haltung*, to use a Brechtian category, as a mode of transmitting an unfamiliar philosophical teaching. This is certainly an unfamiliar kind of political science: it seeks to impart not only an integral knowledge of the structure of the most explosively controversial political situations – revolutions in the order of human things – but also those subjective virtues and dispositions which could inflect the vectors of change. Machiavelli teaches a radicalised form of practical reason, oriented to goals with different time horizons: from the most immediate politics of individual survival and aggrandisement, to projects that could only come to fruition long after one is dead.

The strangely inconclusive nature of Machiavelli's historical judgements and practical counsels make his teachings difficult to summarise. There is no substitute for reading them with open eyes. As we have seen, his fundamental political outlook can seem divided: although he conjures up immense possibilities of political innovation, he is also rightly known as a cold disabuser of utopian illusions. Dismissing 'the many who have imagined republics and principalities that have never been seen or known to exist in truth', he writes that his concern will be to go directly to 'the effectual truth of the thing' and not to our imaginary, enabling fantasies.[20] But while this effectual truth establishes a threshold of historical plausibility, it never functions in his texts as an absolute limit on thought, bolting it to what merely exists. It is more like a sieve, subjecting the most radical proposals to a rigorous criterion of immanence. The notorious anti-utopian formulations of Engels or Lenin convey an approximate sense of Machiavelli's intention here. As this parallel to a later revolutionary tradition suggests, the ban on imagining a new republic is lifted on the condition that one does not shy away from thinking through the hard measures that accompany its origins. This, according to Machiavelli, is very difficult: 'For the greatness of the thing partly terrifies men, so that they fail in their first beginnings.'[21]

IV

The history of turning to Machiavelli to interrogate the structure of the present goes back to the seventeenth century. Commentaries on this figure from Bacon, Harrington or Spinoza – as from Bayle, Montesquieu, Voltaire or

Rousseau – are moments in the intellectual history of the emergence of a politico-philosophical consciousness of modernity. For each of these thinkers, Machiavelli opened the door to an uninhibited exploration of the core problems of this new condition: the future of Christianity, the possibility of republican government, the limits of popular Enlightenment, the decadence and renewal of civilisations, the problematic status of moral and legal limits to the use of political power.

Hegel and Fichte form an intermediate episode between this early modern Machiavellian moment and a later twentieth-century one. German idealism in the Napoleonic age turned to Machiavelli with new concerns, galvanised by the imminent liquidation of the German state. A formulation from Carl Schmitt captures the spirit of this moment, and establishes a crucial focal point for the twentieth-century reception. For Schmitt, the actuality of Machiavelli is vindicated in the situation of 'the ideological defensive', when it becomes imperative to think through the experience of historic defeat.[22]

The nineteenth century witnessed a long decline in this specific genre of reading and commenting on Machiavelli. Outside Italy, he was by and large relegated to the status of a colourful Renaissance period piece, or a distant predecessor of *Realpolitik*. Gramsci offered an intriguing explanation for this hiatus: the nineteenth-century elevation of 'society' as the master category of the order of human things had eclipsed the previous centrality of political categories; with this epistemic break Machiavelli, the great teacher of the art of politics, was supposedly made obsolete by a new understanding of the laws and dynamics of social development. With the dawning of the Age of Extremes in the twentieth-century there came a return, as figures across the political spectrum addressed the new orders emerging from the crisis of liberal-conservative constitutionalism and the interstate system that had been based upon it. In the inter-war era, reading Machiavelli on the origins and fate of the European political world was a notable current in the establishment of political science as an academic discipline, in a context redefined by the roughly simultaneous emergence of Bolshevik and Fascist states.

In what respect did Machiavelli stand out, in comparison to Hobbes and Spinoza, as a theorist of modernity? All three came back into intellectual contention during this period, but in one decisive respect Machiavelli was unique: both Hobbes and Spinoza were contemporaries of a Europe-wide civil-religious war and the central goal of their politicaltheological treatises was neutralisation, or depoliticisation. Machiavelli's career immediately preceded this era of European thought and his reflections on politics and nature were not subjected to this prime directive of pacification. Early twentieth-century encounters with Machiavelli were the occasion for reflections on a horizon beyond liberalism. Forming an arc across the political map, Carl Schmitt, Wyndham Lewis, Leo Strauss, Benedetto Croce, Raymond Aron and Antonio Gramsci, in their own manner, all identified the century as Machiavellian. Others, situated both before and after this period, belong in the same story of theoretical awakening: Maurice Joly from the late nineteenth century, Isaiah Berlin and Louis Althusser from the late twentieth.

V

While the scholarly standard of more recent English-language discussions of Machiavelli and his legacy often exceeds that of these earlier, less exegetical readings, there has arguably been a drop in the appreciation of crucial facets of his thought: those which cannot be so easily pressed into the mould of civic republicanism or of a value-neutral conception of political science. Exhuming these antecedents could provide useful points of entry into reading Machiavelli today. Within the twentieth-century constellation, two studies stand out as sobering reflections on the catastrophic ideological bankruptcies of their time. In his *Thoughts on Machiavelli*, published at the height of the Cold War, Leo Strauss proposed that the most consequential reading of this author must begin with the supposedly naïve assumption that he was a teacher of revolutionary gangsterism.[23] With perhaps a touch of irony, he added that this was a view of things that was against everything America stood for, and by implication could be considered the direct intellectual ancestor of Communism.

For Strauss, the Florentine was the philosophical founder of a modernity whose destiny was the reduction of human nature to the raw material of a techno-politics. Machiavelli's maxim – 'make everything new'[24] – governs a spiritual dispensation that culminated in the revolutionary tyrannies of the twentieth century. Strauss suggested that the West had to relearn from the Italian source the radical art of setting into motion and turning back great historical waves. The task at hand was a long-term project of restoring limits on human enterprise, wisely insisted upon by the classics of ancient political philosophy, as well as by otherwise antithetical Scriptural traditions – the two modes against which Machiavelli had erupted in rebellion. For this it was necessary to construct asylums in which ancient modes of thought could be regenerated, to oppose the onslaught of demotic mass mobilisations of all ideological stripes. The hope was that a new generation of leaders might be inspired to hold the fort against the nihilist consequences of modernity. For the first few decades of the postwar era, the prospects for such a conservative revolution looked dim, but one could take heart by learning from the enemy: 'All unarmed prophets, he says, have failed. But what is he if not an unarmed prophet? How can he reasonably hope for the success of his enormous venture… if unarmed prophets necessarily fail?'[25]

Gramsci's 'The Modern Prince' offered an assessment of Machiavelli's contemporary relevance at a tangent to this one.[26] The former head of a revolutionary party, a political prisoner under Mussolini, the Sardinian was an unarmed prophet *par excellence*. But for Gramsci, far from being the theorist of a victorious march of modernity, Machiavelli was the strategist of reactivating defeated radical causes 'from scratch'. The epochal problem to be deciphered was the European revolution that had failed to materialise. This was no arbitrary projection: the decline of urban republics that Machiavelli confronted was indeed a plausible precedent to his own effort to think through the catastrophic defeat of the European working classes in the age of Fascism and Fordism. For Gramsci, Machiavelli provided the intellectual model of how to conduct a harsh strategic reckoning in the midst of such devastation, as preparation for a very long-term reconstitution of collective praxis through intellectual and material rearmament. This is what he called hegemony. The guiding question of his thoughts on Machiavelli was, accordingly, 'When can the conditions for awakening and developing a national-popular collective will be said to exist?'[27]

Like Strauss, Gramsci was struck by the duality in Machiavelli's thought between a focus on the necessity of tyrannical revolutionary force and an alternative conception of agency as a project of spiritual warfare, slowly unfolding over the course of generations. Christianity was the first religion of unarmed prophecy, the first movement of the war of position. The latter conception of politics manifested itself in a mode of writing addressed simultaneously to the disparate, unreconciled elements of the present generation and to a distant, more sympathetic posterity. For a figure who is often thought to have held that the glory of victory was the sole animating passion of a life of politics, Machiavelli seems to have been unduly preoccupied with how a whole mode of authority 'little by little, and from generation to generation, may be led to disorder'. Machiavelli articulated the ethical imperative that sustains long-term projects of instauration, transvaluation, revolution.

> 'For it is the duty of the good man to teach others the good that you could not work because of the malignity of the times or of fortune, so that when many are capable of it, someone of them more loved by heaven will be able to work it.'[28]

The appeal to less corrupt, future generations is alien to contemporary sensibilities. As a result the political significance of this mode of address in some of the great works of early modern thought is often missed.[29] Such lines speaks to a virtue that has suffered a drastic loss of actuality – namely, fidelity to a cause, even when its great sustaining illusions have been lost. Teaching the Great Method of political innovation was the only ethical imperative that this notorious amoralist seems to have taken seriously.

VI

What does the opposition and diversity of Machiavelli interpretations within this conjuncture suggest? Certainly, the always problematic status, if not the relativity, of even the most compelling political outlooks on one's own times. But also how such partisan commitments are inseparable from the will to discover the effectual truth of the historical situation in which we find ourselves. A formulation from Gramsci pinpoints the open-ended nature of the kind of political theory needed for historical orientation under present circumstances: 'it is necessary', he wrote, 'to develop a theory and technique of politics which… might be useful to both sides in the struggle'.[30] Reading Machiavelli can offer an education in how to probe the fundamentals of one's own allegiances without abandoning hope or succumbing to illusions. Famously his own commitments were themselves obscure: for all the occasional vehemence of his diction, he rarely betrayed any exclusive allegiances to either princes or republics, ruling classes or multitudes, or even ancient as opposed to present times.

Machiavelli's equanimity – 'pessimism of the intellect' – should be distinguished from that spirit of resignation which prevails in times of restoration. After denouncing the errors of false hope in one chapter of the *Discourses*,[31] he turns around in another to offer the following advice on why we should stay with defeated causes, even when we could easily profit by joining the winning side.

> 'Men can second fortune, but not oppose it… they can weave its warp but not break it. They should indeed never give up, for, since they do not know its end and it proceeds by oblique and unknown ways, they have always to hope, not to give up in whatever fortune and in whatever travail they may find themselves.'[32]

There is a long history of commenting on Machiavelli as a theorist of the present as transitional conjuncture, one that needs to be understood in order to bring into focus the lines of a productive contemporary assessment. Reading Machiavelli today opens up the possibility of beginning to develop a radical strategic orientation to some of the core problems of the coming century: the future of the world market, that of the inter-state system and even, in the coming bio-technological age, that of human nature itself. We lack a conception of politics even remotely adequate to the scale of the dangers and possibilities that lie ahead. The present inability and unwillingness to consider – *sanza alcuno rispetto* – a transcendence of the dominant form of state and society is potentially a very perilous situation. For it is arguable that a lot would have to change even to maintain the essentials of this system through another era of crisis and transition.

The problem Machiavelli raises is that discovering the effectual truth of our historical situation requires a radical engagement. The transformability of human conditions cannot be gauged without interrogating the subject that is the imputed bearer of this project. For Gramsci, this subjective element in revolutionary theory was 'a peak inaccessible to the enemy camp'.[33] In relation to the operative political calculus of historically static times, there is an irreducible moment of such subjective 'arbitrariness' involved in adopting adversarial stances that presuppose the possibility of barely conceivable transformations. In his *Discourses on Livy*, Machiavelli brought to light the role played by this irrepressible negativity in the emergence of new historical realities.

> 'Human appetites are insatiable, for since from nature
> they have the ability and the wish to desire all things,
> and from fortune the ability to achieve few of
> them, there continually results from this a discontent in
> human minds and a disgust with the things they possess.
> This makes them blame the present times, praise the
> past and desire the future, even if they are not moved to
> do this by any reasonable cause.'[34]

The negativity of this observational stance raises problems that are extremely difficult to resolve empirically and so perhaps should be considered as philosophical. Are there privileged political positions for observing one's own historical situation? Does the polemical nature of political judgement always do violence to the ironies of history – or conversely, when does understanding a historical situation depend upon precisely this polemical framing of friend and enemy? What viable conception of historical alternatives controls the denunciation of existing conditions? When is the effectual truth grasped in political struggle against the current, and when does it come from floating downstream, away from the immediacy of practice? These are properly philosophical questions Machiavelli raises about politics, which now must be transformed into practical positions. 'Have we got to be lucky?' Brecht writes in his poem, *To a Waverer*,

> 'This you ask.
> Expect No other answer than your own.'

NOTES.
1. Carl Schmitt, 'Das Zeitalter der Neutralisierungen und Entpolitisierungen' (1929), in *Positionen und Begriffe im Kampf mit Weimar-Genf-Versailles*, 1923–1939, Berlin 1988, p. 120.

2. See Francis Mulhern, *Culture/Metaculture*, London, 2000; Stefan Collini, 'Culture Talk', *NLR* 7, January–February 2001; Mulhern, Beyond Metacultue', *NLR* 16, July–August 2002; Collini, 'Deafending Cultural Criticism', *NLR* 18, November–December 2002; Mulhern, 'What is Cultural Criticism?', *NLR* 23, September–October 2003; Stefan Collini, 'On Variousness; and on Persuasion', *NLR* 27, May–June 2004.

3. Louis Althusser, *Machiavelli and Us*, London 2000, p. 7.

4. Tocqueville, letter to Corcelle, 19 October 1839, *Oeuvres complètes* xv, Paris 1951, p. 139.

5. Niall Ferguson, 'Going Critical: American Power and the Consequences of Fiscal Overstretch', *National Interest*, Fall 2003.

6. Niccolò Machiavelli, *Discourses on Livy*, Book ii, ch. 19, trans. Harvey Mansfield and Nathan Tarcov, Chicago 1996, p. 172.

7. For a brilliant discussion of the problem of the 'break' that initiates modernity, see Fredric Jameson, *A Singular Modernity: Essay on the Ontology of the Present*, London 2002.

8. *Discourses*, Book i, Preface, p. 5.

9. *Discourses*, Book ii, Preface, p. 123. A formulation from Fredric Jameson illuminates the politico-epistemological problems Machiavelli confronted: 'Writers tend to organize the events they represent according to their own deeper schemas of what Action and Event seem to be; or. . .

they project their own fantasies of interaction onto the screen of the Real'. Jameson, *Brecht and Method*, London 1998, p. 27.

10. *Discourses*, Book iii, ch. 29, p. 277.

11. *Discourses*, Book iii, ch. 21, p. 263.
12. Machiavelli was an unusual humanist, if indeed he was one, for he was not averse to calling the peak of virtue 'inhuman'. What is the significance of this frightening word of praise in the Machiavellian lexicon? Roughly the same teaching is conveyed in a steely verse from the *Tao Te Ching*: 'Exterminate benevolence, discard righteousness: the people will be a hundred times better off.'

13. *Discourses*, Book i, ch. 17, p. 47; ch. 18, p. 51; ch. 26, p. 61.

14. Jean-Jacques Rousseau, *The Social Contract*, Book ii, p 163; from *The Basic Writings*, Trans. David Cross, Indianapolis 1987.

15. *Discourses*, Book iii, p. 275.

16. Machiavelli, *The Prince*, ch. 3, trans. Harvey Manfield and Nathan Tarcov, Chicago 1998. Those who, like Negri, see Machiavelli's thought as infused with an exultant enthusiasm, miss the dialectic by which such moments emerge out of a drier intelligence. See Antonio Negri, *Insurgencies, Constituent Power and the Modern State*, Minnesota 1999.

17. *Discourses*, Book i, Preface, p. 6; ch. 32, p. 70.

18. Althusser, *Machiavelli and Us*, p. 15.

19. *Discourses*, Book i, ch. 33, p. 71.

20. *The Prince*, ch. 15, p. 61.

21. *Discourses*, Book i, ch. 55, p. 112.

22. Carl Schmitt, *The Concept of the*

Political, Chicago 1996, p. 66.

23. Leo Strauss, *Thoughts on Machiavelli*, Glencoe, il 1959, p. 13.
24. *Discourses*, Book i, ch. 26, p. 61.

25. Strauss, *Thoughts on Machiavelli*, p. 84.

26. Antonio Gramsci, 'The Modern Prince', in *Selections from the Prison Notebooks*, New York 1972.

27. Gramsci, 'Modern Prince', p.130.

28. *Discourses*, Book iii, ch. 8, p. 238; Book ii, Preface, p. 125.

29. Fleeing from the fascist storm, Brecht offered the following guidelines for an art of writing in dark times: 'to equip a work to stand the test of time, on the face of it a "natural" aim, becomes a more serious matter when the writer has grounds for the pessimistic assumption that his ideas may find acceptance only in the long-term. The measures, incidentally, that one employs to this end must not detract from the topical effect of the work. The necessary epic touches applied to things which are "self-evident" at the time of writing lose their value as v-effects after this time. The conceptual autarchy of the works contains an element of criticism: the writer is analysing the transience of the concepts and observations of his own times.' April 24, 1941, *Bertolt Brecht Journals*, trans. Hugh Rorrison, London 1994, p. 145.

30. Gramsci, 'Modern Prince', p. 136.

31. *Discourses*, Book ii, ch. 27, p. 193

32. *Discourses*, Book ii, ch. 29, p. 199.

33. Gramsci, 'Problems of Marxism', *Prison Notebooks*, p. 462.

34. *Discourses*, Book ii, Preface, p. 125.

Ayreen Anastas/Rene Gabri – 16Beaver
16 Beaver Street is the address of a space initiated and run by artists to create and maintain an ongoing platform for the presentation, production, and discussion of a variety of artistic, cultural, economic, and political projects. It is the point of many departures and arrivals. 16Beaver is an independent self-sustaining project. The residents maintain the space by using it as their place of life/work/activities. Residents include Ayreen Anastas and Rene Gabri. See www.16beavergroup.net

Gopal Balakrishnan is an editor of *New Left Review*, and is a Rockefeller Resident Fellow on the Other Globalizations programme at the University of California, Santa Cruz's Center for Cultural Studies. He is the author of *The Enemy: An Intellectual Portrait of Carl Schmitt* (Verso, 2000), editor of *Debating Empire* (Verso, 2003), and the co-editor, with Benedict Anderson, of *Mapping the Nation* (Verso, 1996). A new collection of essays is forthcoming from Verso in 2007.

Michael Blum was born in 1966 in Jerusalem and lives and works in Vienna. Blum's work deals with history, specifically political history. His text for *Make Everything New*, 'The Three Failures', is a transcript of a recent video work, and serves as a starting point for a reflection on the failure of the three definitive ideologies of the twentieth century, which take us on a journey from Riga to Malmö in Sweden and then to New York. He has shown widely in Europe and the US. See www.blumology.net

AA Bronson was born in Vancouver in 1946 and lives and works in Toronto and New York. Together with Felix Partz and Jorge Zontal he formed General Idea in 1969, and they worked collaboratively until their deaths in 1994. General Idea founded Art Metropole, an organisation devoted to collecting, publishing and distributing artists' books, multiples, audio and video. Since 1994 AA Bronson has worked as a solo artist and has had many international solo and group exhibitions. He is Executive Director of Printed Matter in New York, an independent non-profit organisation founded in 1976 by artists and art workers with the mission to foster the appreciation, dissemination, and understanding of artists' books and other artists' publications. He has also built up a practice as a healer. See www.aabronson.com

Maria Eichhorn was born in 1962 in Bamberg and lives and works in Berlin. From the beginning, Eichhorn's work has included collaboration with individuals and groups of people. Her work develops layered and complex relationships between the symbolic and the real, between the literal and the metaphorical. The artist has throughout her body of work focused on the economic aspect of art-making and questions the role of capital in artistic work and the status of the object in the work of art. She is not aiming to provide concrete answers, but, conversely, declares the value of non-productivity and the indefinable nature of artwork.

Factotum was formed in April 2001 by two retired circus performers Stephen Hackett and Richard West to run guided tours and a modern dance programme. Since then Factotum has diversified and now publishes a monthly newspaper *The Vacuum*, runs a choir specialising in communist and corporate repertoire and publishes books sometimes. In 2005 fortune shone upon the organisation and it was awarded a prize by the Paul Hamlyn Foundation which it intends to spend on a trip to Madagascar. See www.factotum.org

Dmitry Gutov was born in 1960 in Moscow where he lives and works. He is a founding member of The Lifshitz Institute which is a collective initiative formed in the early 1990s in Moscow. The Lifshitz Institute actively recalls Marxist-Leninist aesthetics through a re-reading of the theoretical legacy of Michael Lifshitz. The Institute sees his engagement in the critique of Modernism as important and valuable, since it is not only limited to the investigation of movements within the history of art, but it is also includes a broad analysis of the value system of an evolving modern society. The poetic criticism implied with Gutov's Lifshitz Institute is a reflection on the daily realities of Russia. With an attempt to map an island of critical engagement, the collective questions the potential for sharing collective values in the hostile climate of rampant neo-liberalism. See www.gutov.ru

Aleksandra Mir was born in 1967 in Lubin, Poland; she is a citizen of Sweden. And currently lives in New York, US and Palermo, Sicily. Mir's works often take the form of social processes that are open for anyone who wishes give the work meaning. The work of art is an exercise that operates in everyday life; a humanistic and playful organism with a large social appetite. The work's course of events is often started by Mir as a situation-bound juncture between specific events, and the work's location. From this starting point the discussion is extended to more general conditions like traditions, norms and categorisation. See www.aleksandramir.info

Sarah Pierce was born in 1968 in Connecticut, US, and lives and works in Dublin. Over the past four years she has developed The Metropolitan Complex – a project that taps into locality, using a variety of platforms, including talks, papers, exhibitions, and archives – that often open up these structures to the personal and the incidental. Recent projects include *The Meaning of Greatness*, curated by Grant Watson at Project Arts Centre, Dublin 2006; *Archivo Paralelo*, Sala Rekalde, Bilbao 2005; *You Can't Cheat an Honest Man*, PS1/MoMA, New York 2004; and *Paraeducation Department* with Annie Fletcher at Witte de Witte/TENT, Rotterdam, 2004. In 2005, she was one of seven artists who represented Ireland in the 51st Venice Biennale. She regularly publishes *The Metropolitan Complex Papers*, a series of transcribed discussions, and is currently Research Associate in Forms of Curating and Documentation at Interface, University of Ulster, Belfast. She is co-curator with Grant Watson of *Enthusiasm!*, a series of radio programmes on the theme of communism, with Resonance FM for the Frieze Art Fair (October 2006). See www.themetropolitancomplex.com

CK Rajan was born in Kerala in 1960 and studied Fine Art at the University of Kerala, and the University of Hyderabad. During the 1980s he was a member of the Radical Group. His exhibitions include the solo shows, *Mild Terrors* (1995) and *White Prisons* (2004), and various international group shows and workshops. He has published two collections of writings, *Hitler On A Train To Banarus* and *Socrates' Indian Assignment*, the illustrated notebooks *Mad Furniture, Pyschic Objects* and *A Theological Note Book On Flower and Fauna*. He is currently working on the exhibition *Commodities*.

Raqs Media Collective
Raqs (Monica Narula, Jeebesh Bagchi, Shuddhabrata Sengupta) is a collective of media practitioners that works in art practice, new media, film-making, photography, media theory & research, writing, criticism and curation. Raqs Media Collective is the co-initiator of *Sarai: The New Media Initiative*, (www.sarai.net) a programme of interdisciplinary research and practice on media, city space and urban culture at the Centre for the Study of Developing Societies, Delhi. Members of the collective are resident at the Sarai Media Lab, Delhi, where they work on projects interpreting the city and urban experience; make

cross-media works; collaborate on the development of software; design and conduct workshops; administer discussion lists; edit publications; write, research and co-ordinate several research projects and public activities of Sarai. They are co-editors of the *Sarai Reader* series. See www.raqsmediacollective.net

Dont Rhine is a founding member of the audio activist group Ultra-red. Launched in 1994, the Los Angeles-based Ultra-red is made up of political organisers from different social movements who collaborate together with and as artists and musicians. Rhine has been a labour activist and an AIDS activist. See www.ultrared.org

Martha Rosler was born in Brooklyn, New York. She works in video, photo-text, installation, and performance, and writes criticism. Her work engages with gender and everyday life, the media, architecture and the built environment. She has exhibited at Documenta, in Kassel, the Whitney biennial, the ICA, London, the Museum of Modern Art, New York, the Dia Center for the Arts, New York and many other international venues. Rosler has authored ten books, whose subjects range from explorations of cookery to imagery of women in Russia, and to exploring responses to repression, crisis, and war. She teaches at the Mason Gross School of the Arts at Rutgers University, in New Brunswick, New Jersey. See www.martharosler.net

Rob Stone is Senior Research Fellow in the Department of Art, Philosophy and Visual Culture at Middlesex University. His current research focuses on the relationship between fine art, architecture and sound. His first book, *Auditions: Architecture and Aurality*, will be published by The MIT Press in 2007.

Alberto Toscano is a lecturer in sociology and a member of the Centre for the Study of Invention and Social Process at Goldsmiths College. He is the author of *Theatre of Production, Philosophy and Individuation Between Kant and Deleuze*, 2006. He is the author of articles on Schelling, Simondon and Badiou, as well as the co-editor of *Alain Badiou's Theoretical Writings* and *On Beckett*. His current research focuses on the link between contemporary ontology and the idea of communism.

Grant Watson is a curator and writer born in Gloucester in 1967. He lives in Antwerp where he works at the MUHKA. He was the Curator of Visual Arts at Project Arts Centre in Dublin from 2001 to 2006 and during this time he worked with a range of artists and artist groups including General Idea, Bojan Sarcevic, Gerard Byrne, Sarah Pierce, Klaus Weber, Martha Rosler, Heather Allen and Goshka Macuga. His projects relating to communism include the exhibition *Communism* (Project) *Make Everything New* (Book Works / Project) and *Enthusiasm!* (Resonance Radio / Frieze). He has also worked extensively in the area of contemporary Indian Art, co-curating exhibitions with the Indian curator Suman Gopinath such as *Drawing Space: Contemporary Indian Drawing* (inIVA, London), *Room for Improvement* (Crafts Museum, New Delhi) and *Mural* (Project, Dublin).

Klaus Weber was born 1967 in Sigmaringen, Germany and lives and works in Berlin. Weber's work focuses on the relationship between the urban environment and the associations between public and political space. In 2003 he undertook a twelve-month residency at Delfina, London, and exhibited Public Foundation LSD Hall at the Frieze Art Fair. The installation functioned as a proposal for a public building with a centre-piece of a crystal glass fountain circulating 'Potentized LSD' allowing the viewer to 'notice the weirdness of daily life which through repetition has lost its meaning'. Weber's fixation with the role of public space began a major collaborative political film project entitled *A-Clips*, 35mm short films tied to a specific moment in Berlin. The project was later taken to London and New York. See www.k-weber.com.

Wu Ming
In 1994, hundreds of European artists, activists and pranksters adopted a shared identity, Luther Blissett and started to raise hell in the cultural industry. As a five year plan, they worked together to tell the world a great story, create a legend, give birth to a new kind of folk hero. Written as a final contribution to the project by four Bologna-based members, the novel *Q* was published in 1999. In January 2000, the four authors of *Q* were joined by a fifth, and Wu Ming was born. 'Wu Ming' is a Chinese word, meaning either 'anonymous' or 'five names', depending on how you pronounce the first syllable. The name was chosen both as a tribute to dissidence and a rejection of the cult of celebrity. This project, albeit more focused on literature and storytelling in a narrower sense of the word, is no less radical than the old one. *54*, a novel by Wu Ming, was published in 2006. See www.wumingfoundation.com

FOR FURTHER READING / INFORMATION

All contributors to *Make Everything New – A Project on Communism* were invited to compile a selection of texts, books, essays, weblinks and projects that are relevant for communism in general or for their own thinking about the term now. The following list is the outcome of that invitation.

Ayreen Anastas/Rene Gabri – 16Beaver

Jean-Luc Nancy, *Inoperative Community*, Discussions in Contemporary Culture #1, Hal Foster (Ed.), Dia Art Foundation, 1987

Michael Blum

Sergei M. Eisentein, *Notes for a Film of Capital*, published by Annette Michelson in *October #2*, New York, 1976

Nazim Hikmet, *Human Landscapes From My Country*, translated from Turkish by Safiye Behar, Persea Books, New York, 2002

Hannah Arendt, *The Human Condition*, The University of Chicago Press, Chicago, 1958

Charity Scribner, *Requiem for Communism*, The MIT Press, Cambridge MA, 2003

www.marx.org

The Wall Street Journal, New York

AA Bronson

AA Bronson, 'Myth as Parasite/Image as Virus: General Idea's Bookshelf 1967-197'", *The Search for the Spirit: General Idea 1968-1975*, Art Gallery of Ontario, Toronto, 1997

AA Bronson, *Negative Thoughts*, Museum of Contemporary Art, Chicago, 2001

AA Bronson, 'Copyright, Cash, and Crowd Control: Art and Economy in the Work of General Idea', *General Idea Editions: 1967-1995*, Blackwood Gallery, Toronto, 2003

AA Bronson. 'Documenta Sex', *The Next Documenta Should be Curated by an Artist*, e-flux, New York, 2004

Guy Debord, *La Société du Spectacle*, Paris 1967, translated as *The Society of the Spectacle*, Black & Red 1977. The new translation by Donald Nicholson-Smith (Zone Books, 1994) is supposed to be a big improvement on the old Black & Red version, which was the first English translation... but I still have my trusty Black & Red.

General Idea, *Menage à Trois*, Art Metropole, Toronto, 1978

General Idea, *The Getting into the Spirits Cocktail Book from the 1984 Miss General Idea Pavillion*, self-published, Toronto, 1980

General Idea, *FILE Megazine: General Idea's 1984 and the 1968-1984 FILE Retrospective, Vol. 6, Nos. 1 & 2*, The Vancouver Art Gallery/Art Official Inc., Vancouver/Toronto, 1984 (Note: many of General Idea's

writings from various issues of their *FILE Megazine* [1972-1989] can be found in this issue. In particular, note: 'Glamour', reproduced from the Autumn 1975 issue, and 'Three Heads are Better', reproduced from the Summer, 1978 issue. Many of the writings deal, directly or indirectly, with ideas of collaboration, communalism, authorship and copyright).

General Idea, '"How our mascots love to humiliate us...": Revelations from the doghouse', *General Idea 1968-1984*, Stedelijk Van Abbemuseum, Eindhoven, 1984

General Idea. *General Idea's Pharma©opia*, Centre d'Art Santa Monica, Barcelona, 1992

General Idea. *XXX Voto*, S.L. Simpson Gallery/Galerie René Blouin, Toronto/Montreal, 1995

Temporary Services, *Group Work: A Compilation of Quotes About Collaboration from a Variety of Sources and Practices*, self-published, Chicago, April 2002, or just about any of their publishing projects, and in fact the very fact of their publishing endeavour: http://www.temporaryservices.org/booklets.html

Maria Eichhorn

www.eustonmanifesto.org

Jacques Derrida, *Spectres de Marx*, Galilee, Paris 1993

Simon Sheikh (ed.), *Capital (It Fails Us Now)*, b_books, Berlin, 2006

Maria Eichhorn, Maria Eichhorn Aktiengesellschaft / Maria Eichhorn Public Limited Company, Documenta11, Kassel, 2002

Maria Eichhorn, *CAMPUS No. 1, Politische Mundigkeit, Political Responsibility, Emancipazione Politica*, Walther König Verlag, Cologne, 2005

Factotum

Donald Barthelme, *60 Stories*, 1995 (in particular 'Paraguay','A City of Churches' and 'I Bought a Little City')

Søren Kierkegaard, *Either / Or*, 1843 (in particular 'Crop Rotation')

François, Duc de la Rochefoucauld, *Maxims*, 1678

Italo Calvino, *Invisible Cities*, 1974

John Wyndham, *The Day of the Triffids*, 1951

Dmitry Gutov

Karl Marx, 'Private Property and

Communism' in: *Economic and Philosophical Manuscripts of 1844*, http://www.marxists.org/archive/marx/works/1844/manuscripts/comm.htm

Karl Marx and Friedrich Engels, 'Proletarians and Communism' in: *The German Ideology*, 1845. http://www.marxists.org/archive/marx/works/1845/german-ideology/ch01d.htm

Karl Marx and Friedrich Engels, *The Communist Manifesto*, 1848, http://www.marxists.org/archive/marx/works/1848/communist-manifesto/index.htm

Mikhail Lifshitz, *Mikhail Lifshitz. The Philosophy of Art of Karl Marx*, Critic's Group, New York, 1938. Republished by Pluto Press, London, 1973, 1976

Mikhail Lifshitz, 'Leninist Criticisms', 'A Forced Reply', 'How Refutations are Written' and 'Literature and the Class Struggle' in: *Literature and Marxism. A controversy by soviet critics*, Angel Flores (Ed.), Critic's Group, New York, 1938

Mikhail Lifhsitz. 'Karl Marx and Present-Day Culture', In: *Karl Marx and modern philosophy*, Progress Publishers, Moscow, 1968, pp. 143-181

Text archive of works by Mikhail Lifshitz in Russian, http://www.gutov.ru/lifshitz/index.htm

Andrei Platonov, *The Foundation Pit*, 1930, Northwestern University Press, Evanston IL, 1994. Online version Russian original http://ilibrary.ru/text/1010/index.html

Aleksandra Mir

www.utne.com/webwatch/2004_164/news/11375-1.html

www.jimfitzpatrick.ie

www.aleksandramir.info

Sarah Pierce/The Metropolitan Complex

Allen Ginsberg, *The Fall of America: Poems of These States 1965-1971*, City Lights Pocket Poets Series, 1972

Richard Nixon, 'Vietnamization Speech' (3 November 1969) in *Public Papers of the Presidents of the United States, Richard Nixon, 1969*, General Services Administration, National Archives and Records Service, Office of the Federal Register, Washington DC

Raqs Media Collective

For communism http://www.geocities.com/~johngray/

'the site is intended to make communist, anti-capitalist and historical texts available on-line and to link to texts on other sites.'

Self Activity of Wage-Workers Towards a Critique of Representation & Delegation
http://www.geocities.com/CapitolHill/Lobby/2379/leadry.htm

Reflections on Marx's Critique of Political Economy
http://www.geocities.com/CapitolHill/Lobby/2379/critint1.htm

prol-position
http://www.prol-position.net/
'The website is part of an open project discussing and circulating articles from different regions, translated from different languages, and reporting on different spheres of exploitation and proletarian struggle around the world.'

Wikipedia
http://en.wikipedia.org/wiki/Main_Page
The free encyclopedia that anyone can edit.

Dont Rhine

As a member of Ultra-red, I have had the benefit of participating in numerous vital and on-going conversations about histories and praxis of radical social transformation. Given that the artists and organisers involved in Ultra-red come from a variety of social movements, the resulting conversations have drawn on a richly diverse range of experiences with how communities in struggle fight for change. This reading list – eclectic, contradictory, general, specific, reflective, programmatic, philosophical and tactical – includes some of the texts that have informed those conversations over the years. Out of their vocation of discussion within the field of practice, and those desires inexhaustible by our needs, I dedicate this bibliography to my comrades in Ultra-red.

Gioconda Belli, *The Country Under My Skin: A Memoir of Love and War*, Trans. Kristina Cordero, Anchor Books, New York, 2003

Walter Benjamin, 'Surrealism: The Last Snapshot of the European Intelligentsia', in *Selected Writings: Volume 2, 1927-1934*, Trans. Rodney Livingston, Harvard University Press, Cambridge MA, 1999, pp. 207-221

Maurice Blanchot, *The Unavowable Community*, Trans. Pierre Joris, Station Hill Press, Barrytown NY, 1988

Douglas Crimp, *Melancholia and Moralism: Essays on AIDS and Queer Politics*. The MIT Press, Cambridge MA, 2002

Ashwin Desai, *We Are the Poors: Community Struggles in Post-Apartheid South Africa*, Monthly Review Press, New York, 2002

Orlando Fals-Borda, Mohammad Anisur Rahman (Eds.), *Action And Knowledge: Breaking The Monopoly With Participatory-Action Research*, The Apex Press, New York, 1991

Paulo Freire, *The Pedagogy of the Oppressed*, Trans. Myra Bergman Ramos, Continuum International Publishing Group, New York, 2000

Marta Harnecker, *Understanding the Venezuelan Revolution: Hugo Chavez Talks to Marta Harnecker*, Montly Review Press, New York, 2005

John Holloway, *Change the World Without Taking Power: The Meaning*

of Revolution Today, Pluto Press, London, 2005

Jacques Lacan, *The Seminar of Jacques Lacan, Book XVII: The Other Side of Psychoanalysis*, Trans. Russell Grigg, W.W. Norton Press, New York, 2006

Jacob Levenson, *The Secret Epidemic: The Story of AIDS and Black America*, Anchor Books, New York, 2004

Ignacio Martin-Baro, 'Religion as a Form of Psychological Warfare', in *Writings For A Liberation Psychology*, Harvard University Press, Cambridge MA, 1994, pp. 136-150

Antonio Negri, 'Notes on the Evolution of the Thought of the Later Althusser', Trans. Olga Vasile, in *Postmodern Materialism and the Future of Marxist Theory: Essays in the Althusserian Tradition*, David F. Ruccio, et al., (Eds.), Wesleyan University Press, Hanover NH, 1996, pp. 51-68

Antonio Negri, *Books for Burning: Between Civil War and Democracy in 1970s Italy*, Trans. Timothy S. Murphy, Verso, New York, 2005

Rob Stone

AMM, *AMMMUSIC*, 1966

Herbert Biberman, *The Salt of the Earth*, 1953

Cornelius Cardew, *Draft Constitution of the Scratch Orchestra*, 1972

Souleymane Cisse, *Finyé*, 1982

Langston Hughes, *Shakespeare in Harlem*, 1942

Julia Kristeva, *Extraterrestials Suffering For Want of Love*, 1983

William Morris, *News From Nowhere*, 1890

Emmanuel Mounier, *Personalism*, 1950

Pier Paulo Pasolini, *Mamma Roma*, 1962

Vittorio di Sica, *Miracle in Milan*, 1951

AbdouMaliq Simone, *The Visible and Invisible*, 2002

George Steiner, *Proofs and Three Parables*, 1992

Robert Tressell, *The Ragged Trousered Philanthropist*, 1914

Leon Trotsky, *The History of the Russian Revolution*, 1930

Wire, *Outdoor Miner*, 1979

The East River Housing Coop, Lower Manhattan, New York

The Centre for Alternative Technology, Machynlleth, Wales

Alberto Toscano

Theory
Karl Marx, *Economic and Philosophical Manuscripts* (1844); Gyorgy Lukács, *History and Class Consciousness* (1923); Antonio Gramsci, *Pre-Prison Writings* (1910-26); Mao Tse-Tung, 'On Contradiction' (1937); Georges Bataille, *Œuvres complètes, tome I* (1922-40); Jean-Paul Sartre, *The Communists and Peace* (1952-54); Mario Tronti, *Operai e Capitale* (1966); Louis Althusser, *Lenin and Philosophy* (1969); Maurice

Blanchot, *Friendship* (1971); Alain Badiou and François Balmes, *De l'idéologie* (1976); Étienne Balibar, *On the Dictatorship of the Proletariat* (1976); Antonio Negri, *33 Lezioni su Lenin* (1976); Raymond Williams, 'Communism', in *Keywords* (1976); Giorgio Agamben, 'The Idea of Communism', in *The Idea of Prose* (1985); Jacques Rancière, *The Ignorant Schoolmaster* (1987); Geoff Waite, *Nietzsche's Corps/e* (1996); Furio Jesi, *Spartakus. Simbologia della rivolta* (2000); Paolo Virno, *A Grammar of the Multitude* (2002); Stathis Kouvelakis, *Philosophy and Revolution* (2003); Alberto Toscano, 'Communism as Separation', in P. Hallward (ed.) *Think Again* (2004); Alain Badiou and the Cultural Revolution, special issue of *positions: east asia culture critique* (2005)

History and Biography
Karl Marx, *The Civil War in France* (1871); Norman Cohn, *The Pursuit of the Millennium* (1957); Isaac Deutscher, *Stalin* (1966); Patricia W. Romero, *E. Sylvia Pankhurst. Portrait of a Radical* (1987); Stephen Bann (ed.), *The Tradition of Constructivism* (1990); Nanni Balestrini and Primo Moroni (eds.), *L'Orda d'Oro 1968-1977. La Grande Ondata Rivoluzionaria e Creativa, Politica ed Esistenziale* (1997); *The Radical Reformation*, ed. Michael G. Baylor (1991); Michael Denning, *The Cultural Front* (1997); T.J. Clark, *Farewell to an Idea: Episodes from a History of Modernism* (1999); Steve Wright, *Storming Heaven: Class Composition and Struggle in Italian Autonomist Marxism* (2002); Ian Birchall, *Sartre Against Stalinism* (2004); Francesco Dimitri, *Comunismo Magico. Leggende, Miti e Visioni Ultraterrene del Socialismo Reale* (2004); Rossana Rossanda, *La Ragazza del Secolo Scorso* (2005); Moshe Lewin, *The Soviet Century* (2005)

Novels
André Malraux, *Man's Fate* (1933); Nanni Balestrini, *Vogliamo Tutto* (1971); Frederic Tuten, *The Adventures of Mao on the Long March* (1971); Pier Paolo Pasolini, *Petrolio* (1972-75); Luther Blissett, *Q.* (1999) ; Wu Ming, *54* (2002)

Films and documentaries
The Ghost that Never Returns, dir. Abram Room (1929); *Three Songs About Lenin*, dir. Dziga Vertov (1934); *La Marseillaise*, dir. Jean Renoir (1938); *Loin du Vietnam*, collective film (1967); *La Chinoise*, dir. Jean-Luc Godard (1967); *The films of Les Groupes Medvedkine* (1967-74); *The Assassination of Trotsky*, dir. Joseph Losey (1972); *Le Fond de l'Air est Rouge (A Grin Without a Cat)*, dir. Chris. Marker (1977); *Le Tombeau d'Alexandre (The Last Bolshevik)*, dir. Chris. Marker (1992); *Morning Sun*, dir. C. Hinton, G. Barmé, R. Gordon (2003)

Music
Luigi Nono, *Al Gran Sole Carico d'Amore* (1975); Gang of Four, *Entertainment!* (1979); Gruppo operaio 'E Zezi di Pomigliano, *Pummarola Black* (1995)

Websites
Marxists Internet Archive: http://marxists.org/

Il manifesto, quotidiano comunista: http://ilmanifesto.it/

Morning sun, a film and website about the cultural revolution: http://www.morningsun.org/

China & Left Communist Theory: http://www.geocities.com/

chinaleftcom/index.html
Lenin's Tomb, weblog: http://
leninology.blogspot.com/

What in the Hell…, weblog: http://
whatinthehell.blogsome.com/

Marx au XXIeme siècle: L'esprit et la
lettre: http://semimarx.free.fr/

International Library of the
Communist Left: http://www.sinistra.
net/lib/index.html

Colectivo Situaciones: http://www.
situaciones.org/

Grupo Acontecimiento: http://www.
grupoacontecimiento.com.ar/

L'organisation politique: http://
orgapoli.net/

Prelom: http://www.prelomkolektiv.org/

Bureau of Public Secrets: http://www.
bopsecrets.org/

Worker-Communist Party of Iraq:
http://www.wpiraq.net/

Grant Watson

Giorgio Agamben, *The Coming
Community*, Trans. Michael Hardt,
University of Minnesota Press,
Minneapolis, 2003

Giorgio Agamben, *Potentialities,
Collected Essays in Philosophy*, Trans.
Daniel Heller, Stanford University
Press, Roazen, CA, 1999

Giorgio Agamben, *Means Without
Ends, Notes on Politics*, Minnesota
Press, Minneapolis, 2000, p. 111

Louis Althusser, *Lenin and
Philosophy and Other Essays*, Trans.
Ben Brewster, Monthly Review Press,
New York, 2001

Hannah Arendt, *On Revolution*,
Penguin Books, London, 1990

Walter Benjamin, *Understanding
Brecht*, Trans. Anna Bostock, NLB,
London, 1977

Walter Benjamin. *Illuminations*,
Trans. Harry Zohn, Jonathan Cape,
London,1982

Leo Bersani, Ulysse Dutoit, *Forms of
Being Cinema, Aesthetics, Subjectivity*,
British Film Institute, London, 2004

Luther Blissett, 'The Ralph Rumney's
Revenge and other Scams, & How
Luther Blissett Turned a Corporate
Attack on the Multiple Name
into a Marvellous Prank', www.
lutherblissett.net, 2004

Luther Blissett, 'The Luther Blissett
Manifesto, Meeting up with a
Dangerous Character: Luther
Blissett', www.altx.com, 2004

Cornelius Cardew, *Scratch Music*,
Latimer New Dimensions, London,
1972

Cornelius Cardew (Ed.), *Stockhausen
Serves Imperialism*, Latimer New
Dimensions, London, 1974

Cornelius Cardew, 'The Composers
Index, Biographical Notes', www.
w-mids.freeserve.co.uk, 2004

Cornelius Cardew, Dir. Regniez,
Philippe, The Arts Council, London,
1884 (video)

Gilles Deleuze, Félix Guattari,
*Anti-Oedipus Capitalism and
Schizophrenia*, Trans. Robert Hurley,
Mark Seem, and Helen R. Lane, The
Athlone Press, London, 2000

*A Thousand Plateaus Capitalism and
Schizophrenia*, Trans. Brian Massumi,
The Athlone Press, London, 1999

Jacques Derrida, *Specters of Marx
The State of the Debt, the Work of
Mourning, & the New International*,
Trans. Peggy Kamuf, Routledge,
London, 1994

Mahasweta Devi, *Bashai Tudu*, Trans.
Samik Bandyopadhyay and Gayatri
Chakravorty Spivak, Thema, Kolkatta,
2002

Mahasweta Devi, *Mother of 1084*,
Trans. Samik Bandyopadhyay, Seagull
Books, Kolkatta, 1997

Félix Guattari, *Chaosmosis. An
Ethico-Aesthetic Paradigm*, Trans.
Paul Bains and Julian Petanis, Power
Press, Power Institute of Fine Art,
Sydney, 1995

Félix Guattari, *The Guattari Reader*,
Gary Genesko (Ed.), Blackwell
Publishers, Oxford, 1996

Félix Guattari, *Soft Subversions*,
Sylvere Lotringer (Ed.), Trans.
David L. Sweet and Chet Wiener,
Semiotext(e), New York, 1996

Félix Guattari, *The Three Ecologies*,
Trans. Ian Pinder and Paul Sutton,
The Athlone Press, London, 2000

Edward Fox, *Death of a Dissident*,
London: Independent Newspaper,
1992

Eugene Lunn, *Marxism and
Modernism: An Historical Study
of Lukács, Brecht, Benjamin and
Adorno*, University of California
Press, London, 1984

Karl Marx, *Capital. A Critique of
Political Economy*, Trans. Eden &
Cedar Paul, George Allen & Unwin,
London, 1929

David McLellan, *Marxism: Essential
Writings*, Oxford University Press,
Oxford, 1988

David McLellan, *The Thought of Karl
Marx*, The Macmillan Press Ltd.,
London, 1995

Jean-Luc Nancy, *Being Singular
Plural*, Stanford University Press,
Roazen CA, 2000

Wu Ming, 'Why not Show Off About
the Best Things & Tute Bianche', from
Infopool No.7, www.infopool.org.
uk, 2003

'From Multiple Names to Wu Ming',
(text by Antonio Caronio) www.
wumingfoundation.com, 2001

Antonio Negri, *Time for Revolution*,
Trans. Matteo Mandarini,
Continuum, London, 2003

Jaqcues Rancière, *The Politics of
Aesthetics*, Continuum, London, 2005

Martha Rosler, P*ositions in the Life
World*, Catherine de Zegher (Ed.),
Ikon Gallery, Birmingham, 1999

Martha Rosler, *The Monumental
Garage Sale*, VHS Video, exhibition
loop, 30 mins, Electronic Arts
Intermix, London, 1977

Michael Ryan, *Marxism and
Deconstruction, a Critical
Articulation*, John Hopkins University
Press, Baltimore,1986

Gayatri Chakravorty Spivak, *In Other
Worlds. Essays in Cultural Politics*,
Methuin, London, 1987

Stefan Szczelkun, '25 Years from Scratch',
www. Stefan-Szczelkun.org.uk, 1994

Stefan Szczelkun, 'The Scratch
Orchestra', www. Stefan-Szczelkun.
org.uk, 2004

Wu Ming

'Trouble is: no book title re
communism comes to mind. What
kind of books you mean? Essays,
theoretical stuff, Toni Negri etc? We
don't dig that stuff anymore, we got
fed up years ago… :-)'

MAKE EVERYTHING NEW
A Project on Communism

Published by Book Works, London and
Project Arts Centre, Dublin
Distributed by Book Works

Photograph credits
p. 30 Dmitry Gutov: photographs by Konstantin Bokhorov
p. 54 (Top) All rights reserved Revolutionary Communist
Party of Britain (Marxist-Leninist) archives; (bottom)
Courtesy The Modern Institute/Toby Webster Ltd, Glasgow
pp. 74 – 79 Maria Eichhorn: Courtesy Galerie Barbara Weiss,
Berlin,© VG-Bild-Kunst, Bonn, Maria Eichhorn

Book Works would like to thank Gopal Balakrishnan and
New Left Review for permission to reprint 'Future Unknown:
Machiavelli for the Twenty-First Century', which first
appeared in *New Left Review* 32, March – April 2005.

ISBN 1 870699 93 9

Book concept by Grant Watson
Edited by Grant Watson, Gerrie van Noord and Gavin Everall
Design by Secondary Modern
Typeset in *UTOPIA* and Schreibmaschinenschrift
Printed by Drukkerij Imschoot, Ghent

Make Everything New – A Project on Communism is the first
of a new series of nine co-publishing partnerships by Book
Works, entitled *Fabrications*, to be published over the next
three years.

Book Works is supported by the Arts Council England.
Fabrications is supported by Grants for the Arts, Arts
Council of England.

Project Arts Centre is supported by The Arts Council / An
Chomhairle Ealaíon and Dublin City Council.

Cover: CK Rajan, *Seen in Europe, Africa, Japan and the
showrooms of your nearest Pal-Peugot Dealer* (detail), 1992–
1995, collage on paper, 195 x 195 mm

Book Works
19 Holywell Row
London EC2A 4JB
www.bookworks.org.uk

Project Arts Centre
39 East Essex Street
Temple Bar
Dublin 2
www.project.ie